CONCILIUM

Religion in the Eighties

CONCILIUM

Concilium 162 (2/1983): Liturgy

LITURGY:
A CREATIVE TRADITION

Edited by
Mary Collins
and
David Power

English Language Editor
Marcus Lefébure

T. & T. CLARK LTD.
Edinburgh

THE SEABURY PRESS
New York

February 1983
T. & T. Clark Ltd., 36 George Street, Edinburgh EH2 2LQ
ISBN: 0 567 30042 0

The Seabury Press, 815 Second Avenue, New York, NY 10017
ISBN: 0 8164 2442 X

Library of Congress Catalog Card No.: 82-062755

Printed in Scotland by William Blackwood & Sons Ltd., Edinburgh

Concilium: Monthly except July and August.
Subscriptions 1983: UK and Rest of the World £27·00, postage and handling included; USA and Canada, all applications for subscriptions and enquiries about *Concilium* should be addressed to The Seabury Press, 815 Second Avenue, New York, NY 10017, USA.

CONTENTS

Editorial:
Liturgy, A Creative Tradition

THE CHURCH is the subject of liturgical action, and it is the Church which has a twenty-centuries-old tradition of public worship. The central concern of this issue is an examination of creativity as a constitutive element of that liturgical tradition. Three sets of articles contribute to that purpose: foundations, historical investigations, and reflections on the present situation.

In the first of the *foundational articles*, Charles Perrot identifies as the source of Christian creativity in public worship the novel deed of God accomplished in Jesus Christ. From the beginning the Church's celebration of his presence among us announcing the reign of God has had the effect of both breaking down and building up, in the best biblical tradition. Joseph Gelineau's essay shows the complexity of the current liturgical reform, one which is characterised less by spontaneity than by conscious planning to authorise and also to limit liturgical innovation. He notes the operative principles which aim to balance the claims of the received tradition with a flexibility of performance that leaves room for innovations rooted in the real cultural diversity of local churches. Mary Collins examines the charge about a late twentieth century 'ideology of creativity' and looks at the operative obstacles to continuing creativity in the post-conciliar Church.

The *historical investigations* focus on what occurred in the liturgical tradition in three critical periods of social, cultural, and ecclesial transition, moments which are receptive to human inventiveness. Pedro Farnes Scherer stresses the weight of fixed liturgical forms inherited from Judaism which moderated and mediated liturgical innovation even in the apparently fluid post-apostolic period. Charles Pietri examines the compenetration of liturgical, social, and cultural forms effected in Rome in the fourth and fifth centuries as a result of Constantine's public favour of the Church. The unprecedented liturgical forms and the ecclesial consciousness they implied became the very fabric and even the glory of the Roman liturgical tradition. James White looks at an outcropping from the formalised Roman tradition, namely, the trajectory of Free Church worship initiated by radical sixteenth-century reformers and subsequently taken up in ways responsive to the circumstances of nineteenth-century American frontier life.

Five *reflections on present ecclesial experience* complete the investigation of creativity as a constitutive element of the liturgical tradition. Witnesses from four continents point to the kinds of developments which underscore Gelineau's observation: 'Le modele "rite romain" n'existe plus (sauf vestiges).' From Upper Volta Bishop Tatiamne Anselme Sanon writes of values which undergird an African critique of the received tradition and which inspire creativity (not unlike that the Romans of the Constantinian era showed) to generate an authentic African liturgical celebration of the mystery of faith. Paul Puthanangady reports on the progress of the Indian hierarchy's programme for developing an Indian expression of the received liturgical tradition.

From Western Europe Herman Wegman looks at apparently minor liturgical innovations which signal significant new perceptions among European Catholics of their ecclesial identity and mission, meanings which differ from those embodied in the received Roman liturgy. José Aldazábal identifies values and questions in western youth culture which also impinge on the way that the new generation in the oldest established churches of the West wish to celebrate the mystery of Christ. From North America, Francis Sullivan writes as a solitary artist, describing and evaluating the creative person's struggle to fashion something which is faithful to the tradition of public worship, that is, something which will reveal the living God and the Risen Christ in the present moment.

Early in the development of twentieth-century liturgiology Anton Baumstark identified several 'laws of liturgical development' which helped to advance historical studies of the liturgy and to prepare for the conciliar reform. At the end of the century liturgiologists and the worshipping Church seek further critical insight into the rapid development of the tradition of public worship in which we are all participating. This issue, focusing on the creativity which is endemic to a believing and worshipping Church, aims to advance that understanding.

MARY COLLINS
DAVID POWER

PART I

Foundations

Charles Perrot

Worship in the Primitive Church

IN THE words and actions they used in their worship the first Christian communities remained deeply immersed in the Jewish traditions within the Hellenistic world. Prayer and chant, the style of preaching and teaching, the action of baptism and the communal meal had their origin in part in Judaeo-Hellenistic practice. But it is not always easy to work out precisely what derives from this tradition, and for this there are a number of reasons:

(1) The Jewish tradition we are dealing with is still not well known, does not seem very homogeneous and is often difficult to date.

(2) The Christian communities, whether in Palestine or in the diaspora, present a remarkable variation in their attachment to the old tradition. The problem of the relationship between the Torah and the New Covenant comes up in different ways for the Judaeo-Christian groups as it does for the different Helleno-Christian groupings, and yet the Torah's relationship with the New Covenant determined Christian liturgical practice.

(3) Moreover, from the methodological point of view, in the liturgical field as elsewhere explaining a practice by its origin is something that has always to be treated with caution because of the risk of disguising the radical changes that have taken place. Earlier traditions and sources never provide a complete explanation of a given practice in its new form and context.

(4) Finally, we cannot forget the phenomenon of re-Judaisation which quickly took place, even in Helleno-Christian communities (thus Col. 2:16-18, 23). Sometimes the allegedly Jewish origin of this or that Christian practice is merely a secondary historical phenomenon. In this context the account given by the Acts of the Apostles is rightly open to criticism. Writing at what is already a late period (towards AD 80 or 90), its author is in fact trying to link the ideas and the practice of the churches derived from Paul to the 'proto-history' of the Petrine community and finally to Israel itself. Christian practice, too, is made to look as if it derives, almost without a break, from an Israel of which it is presented as the final flowering. The model presented by the scene of Pentecost, like that of the primitive community that was constant in attending the Temple (Acts 2:46, 5:42), demonstrates first of all Luke's theology of the ideal Church, in its link with the starting-point of the people of God. The ritual action taken by Paul according to Acts 21:26 does not really fit in at all with what we know about the apostle

from other sources. In other words, Luke to some extent 'Judaises' the figure of Paul. The tensions and divisions are wiped out to correspond to the situation of the Church at the end of the first century when the threat to the authenticity of the word of salvation meant in effect that one had to go back to the values of earlier times ('The old is good', says Luke 5:39 in contrast to the parallel passage in Mark). But this kind of picture, with a smooth and idyllic development from Israel to the Church, risks disguising what is specific in Christian liturgical practice. Hence, before beginning to evaluate the contribution of the Jewish tradition it is necessary to underline the extent to which Christian practices diverged from the Jewish tradition. There was a break to begin with, which different communities were more or less keenly aware of, but which did not stop them preserving or re-absorbing elements from Jewish worship that had now become Christianised.

In order to gain a proper appreciation of this initial break as well as of this continuity across the break we must not above all project our modern ideas on to the situation as it was then, for example by contrasting a Jewish form of worship that is purely external, ritualistic and formalist with a Christian practice that has become open to the freedom of the Spirit. On this interpretation the Jewish system, laden with hypocrisy, would ultimately collapse before the inwardness of 'worship in the Spirit'. In fact, the scribes of the synagogues, like the people of Qumrân in their admirable hymn of prayer, lived with intensity the religion of the prophets of Israel. The passages from the prophets read in the synagogues of the Pharisaic tradition, from around the second century BC onwards, did not remain a dead letter. A further point is that the process of institutionalisation seems to have taken place at times more quickly in the Church than in the synagogue itself. For example, up till about the ninth century of the Christian era the Jews took care not to write down their customary prayers, using formulations that always remained flexible and open to new ideas, while the text of the Our Father was very rapidly fixed in its double tradition (Luke and Matthew). True, the author of the *Didache* allows more freedom: 'Allow prophets to celebrate the Eucharist as they wish' (*Didache* 10:7). Similarly the attempt at rationalisation undertaken by Paul in the context of Corinth, aimed at 'edification', in other words an ecclesiastical set-up 'in order' (1 Cor. 14:26, 40), in fact precedes the corresponding attempt undertaken in the synagogues in the second century of our era with the aim of unifying Jewish practices which had at this time been enlarged by the legacy of the Temple. Liberty and creativity are not as such the prerogatives of Christianity. Moreover, this kind of facile contrast in fact disguises the profound cleavage that took place between the old covenant of the law and the new covenant of the cross. How can this disjunction be described?

1. THE SEARCH FOR A VOCABULARY

Let us start from an acknowledged fact. The New Testament does not have a word covering precisely what today we mean by Christian worship. During this initial stage words were being looked for to express a new and diverse reality that was not a simple prolongation of the sacrificial worship of yesterday. The new vocabulary of service at table (in Greek *diakonia*) nevertheless tended to become established, while the Greek nouns *latreia* and *leitourgia*, used to describe the old sacrificial worship, seemed at this stage to be rejected or were in need of amendment. They carried too great a resonance of the bloody worship of the Temple (see Rom. 9:4; Luke 1:23) against which the baptist groups, the Judaeo-Christians of the Hellenist type (Acts 6:1) and Jesus himself had protested (John 2:13-21). But the Temple was to be once again evoked among Christians, especially after its destruction in AD 70, but this time radically reinterpreted either christologically (John 2:19-21), or ecclesiologically (Mark 14:58). Similarly, the verb *latreuein* (to render worship) and the corresponding noun came into use again in the Christian vocabulary but given a spiritual qualification which completely transformed them: thus it is a question of worship in the Spirit (Phil. 3:3; Rom. 1:9) and of 'rational worship' or worship shot through with the word (Rom. 12:1: *logikē latreia*). What is involved in these apparent references to worship is simply qualifying the new life of the Christian, not at all describing what today we would include under the heading of worship. The new way of life, under the sign of the Spirit, is no longer divided off from the world in which it is situated: the *disciplina arcani* no longer exists (1 Cor. 14:23). To sum up, as far at least as the New Testament is concerned, we need to avoid talking thoughtlessly of Christian 'worship' as if a word of this type existed at that time to unite within it the diversity of practices which were continually in search of their own identity.

2. NEW TIMES AND NEW PLACES

It is all the more important to notice this last point in that the first Christians deliberately chose expressions which up till then had been used in the context of secular life to designate the ministers of their assembly and the new community rituals. Communities met in private houses, and thus outside any sacred place or area: in the house of Prisca and Aquila (1 Cor. 16:19) or at the home of Nympha (Col. 4:15). Without a doubt such a thing as the Christian 'synagogue' existed in the Judaeo-Christian world (see James 2:2), but before the second century AD Jewish synagogues were specifically not considered sacred places. Moreover, Christians used to meet on 'the first day of the week' (1 Cor. 16:2; Acts 20:7), in other words not during the sacred time of the sabbath. However, a certain sacralisation of time was fairly rapidly to be expressed, helped by expressions like 'the Lord's day' (Rev. 1:10, *Didache* 14:1). The sacred times of the festivals of former times do not seem to have been respected at first, at least not by all the Christian communities, except at the relatively late stage of the Lucan community (which did so with regard to Pentecost). Certainly the Jewish feast of the Passover was always commemorated, but its spiritual significance had now been transformed (1 Cor. 5:7-8). Finally, respect for the sabbath was soon to become a subject of dissension even within the Christian communities. If Judaeo-Christians continued always to respect it (the inference of Matt. 24:20), the Hellenist branch of Jewish Christianity, and soon the Greek Christians who did not succumb to the movement of re-Judaisation mentioned above (Col. 2:16), refused to follow its demands. By recalling Jesus' attitude in this circumstance the Gospels influenced by this Hellenist tradition made this quite plain. This broad rejection of the sacred times and places of the past shows the desire to link Christian 'liturgical' practice from now on to daily life which has now been invaded by the Spirit (Rom. 8 and 12). A similar distance between the former pattern of worship and the new way of life is also shown with regard to those Christian actions that are apparently the closest to former patterns of behaviour. We shall list several of these practices, but unfortunately too rapidly to be able to justify all the considerations that follow.

3. BAPTISM

The history of the Christian action of baptism is one of a continual transformation and of successive re-interpretations. The link with the Jewish tradition in the action of ritual ablution, allowing one to pass from the secular world to the sacred domain, now became a distant one. The same applies to those practices of ritual purity using the water from the cisterns at Qumrân, even if in practice this action was given an interior significance by being a sign of the return of the spirit of holiness. What is termed the baptism of proselytes that sometimes accompanied circumcision remained an action of ritual purity at the time of leaving the world of idolatry, and was hardly practised in first-century Judaism. At the very heart of the Jewish world the real novelty came with John the Baptist and the group or groups that followed him. This time the aim of the action was to proclaim the forgiveness of sins, accompanied obviously by the conversion of the heart. Jesus took up this action only at the start of his ministry, as a sign of the coming reign or kingdom of God. Subsequently the Christian communities re-introduced the practice, though we cannot always say precisely when or how. A diversity of practice was thus known, like that of the Johannine Christians at Ephesus (Acts 18:25-19:7), before the custom gradually prevailed of a single baptism (Eph. 4:5) as a substitute for circumcision. This last action, indicating entry among the people of the covenant, continued to be practised in certain Christian circles (Acts 15:1). Overcoming an apparent hesitation (1 Cor. 1:15-17, 10:1-5), Paul accepted the action of baptism that had now become traditional, but on condition of placing it in the context of the only action that saved, that of the cross of the Risen One. It was no longer the water of baptism that forgave but only the cross of the Saviour: from now on the action of baptism owed its value to this cross on which every person who was baptised was from now on crucified (Rom. 6:3-5). An analogous rectification or re-interpretation was also obtained with the help of a different Christian language, this time by dissociating baptism with water from the baptism of the Spirit (Mark 1:8; Acts 1:5). The starting-point of the saving action is thus considered in terms of the event of the resurrection, now proclaimed by the Spirit. Once again, salvation has its roots in the Lord, by the Spirit of the Risen One, and no longer simply in the water of baptism. As one can see, the history of baptism goes back to the Jewish tradition, and is well within it; but what are really significant are ultimately the breaks in interpretation and understanding in this history, and not the material continuity of a ritual action using water. Everything is old and new at one and the same time, in this 'christologisation' of the actions of the community that decisively indicated what was specific about Christianity.

4. PRAYER

The same applies to prayers and chants in the new community. From now on everything is centred on the person of Christ. Round about AD 111-113 Pliny the younger wrote: '(The Christians come together) on a particular day, before the sun rises, to sing antiphonally a song (*carmen*) in honour of Christ as in honour of a god' (*Letters* x:96:7). The christological hymns of the New Testament are a good example of this, not to mention the doxologies (Phil. 2:6-11; Col. 1:15-20; 1 Tim. 3:16). To these we can add psalm-like compositions like the Benedictus (Luke 1:68-79) or that prayer of Midrashic cast which Luke offers his community as the model of the earliest Christian prayer (Acts 4:24-30). The communities thus pray and sing the Lord Christ with 'psalms and hymns and spiritual songs' (Col. 3:16; Eph. 5:19). It is without doubt difficult to define precisely the different types used here. The psalms in question are apparently new compositions made up for the occasion (1 Cor. 14:26), in the style of the psalms generally composed in the synagogues, both before and after the destruction of the second Temple (cf. the psalms of Solomon on the one hand and the *Piyyutim* of the sabbath and feast-days on the other).

Three points at least mark what is new and distinctively Christian. First, there is an intense christologisation of the compositions made at that time, as is seen again in the canticles of Revelation (Rev. 5:9, 14:3, 15:3). Secondly, the customary prayers of

Judaism are abandoned in favour of placing a value on prayers of a private nature. The monotheist confession of faith of the *Shema Yisrael* (Deut. 6:4), recited by Jews twice or three times a day, is apparently no longer used, and the same goes for the ancient elements of the *Shemoneh 'Esreh* (the Eighteen Benedictions). Of course, the prayer *par excellence* of the synagogue, that is to say the blessing ('Blessed are you, Lord, because . . .' followed by a commemorative theme) is not forgotten: its existence is recalled at the start as well as at the conclusion of the communal meal (1 Cor. 11:24), but nevertheless it came to be supplanted by formulations that up till then had been accepted in the framework of the prayer of asking, of a private or domestic character, of which the Our Father is the perfect example. Moreover, Paul underlines the always important role of the person endowed with the gift of speaking in tongues, that is to say the charism of prayer, provided from now on he expresses himself in language that can be understood: the speaker in tongues is precisely the specialist in these benedictions and thanksgivings or Eucharists to which the believer described as being in the position of an outsider, the 'non-expert', should answer 'Amen' (1 Cor. 14:16).

In the third place let us simply mention gestures of prayer like kneeling and still more proskynesis or prostration reserved until then for the God of the Temple (1 Cor. 14:25). Normally Jewish prayers are said standing, even if in certain cases of private prayer prostration is not unknown (as for example with Rabbi Akiba).

5. THE MEAL

The Christian meal is clearly the place where the christologisation mentioned above reaches its height, even if nearly all the elements of this meal offer certain analogies with Jewish practices of the first century AD. We need mention only the Jewish meals of the sabbath and feast-days, the Essene meals at which the Messianic theme is present, and above all the astonishing meal of the Egyptian Therapeutae mentioned by Philo of Alexandria in his *De vita contemplativa*. With the paschal meal we have the unique example of a Jewish meal having become also the place for readings from the Bible and singing hymns. It is not easy to sum up in a few words the history of the first Christian meals linked as they were to the Jewish tradition while having a radically new content. There are at least two reasons for this: first, these meals seem to have brought together various different Jewish practices in a single community action; second, Christian practice itself seems to have differed appreciably from one community to another.

Three Jewish practices are particularly involved. First, important meals with guests, including the blessing of the bread and that of the cup on sabbaths and feast-days or at the community meals known in the Jewish diaspora, such as the *syndeipna* of the Jewish communities in Rome mentioned by Josephus. Secondly, there is the system of mutual aid attached to each synagogue, under the direction of the top leaders of the Jewish community, with the daily provision for the poor pilgrim and the provision for widows and the poor distributed just before the sabbath. Finally, we should briefly recall everything that comes from the use of the Bible in the sabbath morning service in the synagogues, with its readings, its chants and its homiletic exhortations; or again all the teaching of the scribes concerning how one should behave in terms of the Torah.

The history of the earliest Christian meals directly affects the relationship between these diverse practices, whether they are brought together in the same community celebration or whether they are soon dissociated once again. The *agapes* of mutual aid within the community were to be dissociated from what became known as the eucharistic meal, perhaps from the start of the second century. (Is it already the case in Jude 12?) The liturgical tradition seems to be pretty well stabilised at the time of someone like St Justin when one can already recognise the normal sequence of the reading of the Gospel (the memoirs of the apostles) and that of the prophets, then the homily, the prayers and the gestures over the bread and the wine, followed by the Amen (*Apology* I § 67). A similar sequence is to be found in Acts 20:7-12, linking together the word and the breaking of bread during the night that follows the sabbath. But let us go back a few decades earlier, to a time when the linking together of the three Jewish practices mentioned above, now Christianised, seems very close. This is well shown by the very evolution of the Greek word *diakonia*, which rapidly became fashionable in Christian circles: at one and the same time it meant the service of the new table, the service of mutual aid within the community (and hence what for us has become the collection), and finally the service of the word. The daily *diakonia* or service of the Seven described in Acts 6:1-7 again reflects this close link between the meal and mutual aid within the community, even if the passage in question already evokes a certain distance that had become apparent in the Lucan community between the service of the table and that of the word (Acts 6:4). The combination of the service of the new table and of mutual aid had clearly not been reduced at this time to the simple eucharistic words and gestures which according to custom began and ended the meal. Once again it was necessary to distinguish correctly these significant limits of the 'Lord's Supper' and thus to wait for each other (1 Cor. 11:17-34).

What is thus pre-eminently the community celebration is also that of the new word. The Lord is continually gathering those who are his together, presides at his table and speaks to them once again. An essential role is thus played by the Christian prophets, that is to say the spokesmen and spokeswomen of the Lord, both in the Palestinian communities (Acts 11:27, 15:32) and in the Christian diaspora. There, too, it was a major novelty to give the more important place to this prophetic role taken from Israel's past as against the role of the learned experts who up till then had dominated the synagogues. Among charisms Paul distinguishes what are termed the spiritual charisms, that is to say prayer and prophecy (cf. 1 Cor. 12-14), or more precisely glossolalia or speaking in tongues, now accompanied by an interpretation so that the prayer or the word addressed to God becomes also a word that people can hear, and prophecy, now accompanied by the community charism of discernment, so that the word of Jesus brought by the prophet is also the word of the Church which has been properly sifted and judged. As Jesus' spokesman to the assembled community or God's spokesman on Jesus by the mediation of a scripture that from now on was Christianised, the Christian prophet thus takes on an essential role. It is through him that there takes place that first recollection of what the Lord said, both yesterday and today, sayings soon to be collected by the Christian learned men before becoming what Justin terms the memoirs of the apostles or the 'prophet writings' mentioned in Rom. 16:26 (probably meaning elements of a Gospel). Is it necessary to add that this recollection will take different forms in different communities before resulting in our four canonical Gospels, among others? And each time there re-echoes an understanding that is at one and the same time shared and divergent of him whose presence is proclaimed in the community meal and who is unflaggingly re-presented by means of the word. No doubt yet more considerable differences existed between the various communities, to the point of sometimes forgetting the presence of the cross at the very heart of the community meal: the Eucharist of Christian prophets described in the *Didache* never mentions it once. In these conditions we can understand better the sharp reaction of the apostle decisively planting the cross at the very heart of the celebration of the Risen One: 'You proclaim the Lord's death until he comes' (1 Cor. 11:26). This authoritative interpretation of the Christian meal, with its reference to the past of the crucified one, the present of the Risen One, and the future of the Lord who comes, finally affects all Christian liturgical actions. Beyond all the Jewish practices that have become tangled up and duly reinterpreted, beyond even the language of worship or sacrifice that the apostle has more or less taken up (Rom. 3:35, 12:1), it is here and nowhere else that the most radical novelty of the Christian liturgy is to be found.

At the conclusion of the earliest liturgies the Christians used to cry *Marana Tha*, 'Lord, come', not 'Lord, return', but rather 'Lord, come and look for us' (1 Cor. 16:22; Rev. 22:20; *Didache* 10:6; and see 1 Thess. 4:13-17). By this the Christian is always like the traveller who celebrates the Passover of his liberation. The actions he performs do not simply recall the past of the man of Nazareth, and they do not only fill him with the satisfaction of the spiritual presence of the Risen One, at the risk sometimes of becoming engulfed by a new kind of magic (1 Cor. 10:1-13). What Christians do, baptism along with prayer and the meal along with fasting (Mark 2:20), remain proclamations of the kingdom or reign of God in the expectation of the Lord who is coming. No doubt the three dimensions of past, present and future already partly spanned the worship of the old covenant. Now everything is completely new, in the continuity and the novelty of the Word of God.

Translated by Robert Nowell

Recent Bibliography

E. Käsemann 'Gottesdienst im Alltag der Welt' in *Judentum, Urchristentum, Kirche* ed. W. Eltester (Berlin 1960) pp. 165-171.

E. Käsemann *Perspectives on Paul* (Philadelphia 1971).

S. Lyonnet 'La Nature du culte dans le Nouveau Testament' in *La Liturgie après Vatican II* (Paris 1967) 357-384, also available as 'La nature du culte chrétien' in *Worship and Ritual in Christianity* (Rome 1974) 213-249.

S. Lyonnet 'Le culte spirtuel, Rom 12:1-2' in *Assemblées du Seigneur* 53 (1970) 11-14.

F. Hahn *Der Urchristliche Gottesdienst* (Stuttgart 1970).

C. Perrot 'Le Repas du Seigneur' in *La Maison-Dieu* 123 (1975) 29-46.

E. Schüssler Fiorenza 'Cultic Language in Qumrân and in the New Testament' in *Catholic Biblical Quarterly* 38 (1976) 159-177.

G. W. Buchanan 'Worship, Feasts and Ceremonies in the Early Jewish-Christian Church' in *New Testament Studies* 26 (1979-80) 279-297.

A. Beckwith and others *Influences juives sur le culte chrétien* (Abbaye du Mont César) (Louvain 1981).

H. J. Klauck 'Die Hausgemeinde als Lebensform im Urchristentum' in *Münchener Theologische Zeitschrift* 32 (1981) 1-15.

B

Joseph Gelineau

Tradition—Invention—Culture

A CELEBRATION of the liturgy, being a symbolic action, forms one meaningful whole. No one element within it, of sound, sight or gesture, is independent of the others. So if one element of the rite is altered, the significance of the whole may change.

The reason for the preceding remarks lies in the particular kind of discussion this article will contain. The scientific knowledge we normally reason with is cumulative: we can learn the new maths or a foreign language without unlearning classical maths or forgetting our mother tongue. Where thought and action are concerned, we can change conceptual tools and select the one most suited to the task in hand. But in the order of symbol, the case is very different. If just three notes in a melody or one colour in a picture are altered, the whole work changes. It will be described as 'disfigured' or 'rejuvenated', according to the speaker's taste. If we go to live abroad and become used to different customs in such matters as courtesy, food and free time, when we return home our perception of the manners, cooking and art of our own country will necessarily be different. Or again, if one part of the ritual of Sunday mass is altered, people will say that religion is being changed.

When Vatican II embarked on updating the liturgy, the aim was to reform the Roman rite. Within what tradition had handed down, immutable elements were distinguished from changing elements. Then the latter: language, music, postures, were treated as if they were interchangeable components within the general framework and traditional structures of the Roman rite. But if the Roman rite is shorn of, say, the Latin language, is it still the same symbol?

Fifteen years after the Council's reforms, the picture is by no means homogeneous. Sometimes a pre-Vatican II mentality can still be seen beneath the new rites, which form a kind of veneer. Elsewhere, the framework is that of the prescribed set of rites established by the reform, and the actual living liturgy is a different one, so that there has been a true graft. Most commonly though, there is a 'collage' which is composed of differing elements but leaves no impression that any real rethinking has been done.

This raises the following question: if, like any other symbolic activity, Christian worship can exist, develop, and produce its 'religious' effects only within a specific culture, how does it retain its identity when there is cultural change? How can ever-changing assemblies celebrate it in such a way as to combine authentic remembrance of Jesus Christ and true present enactment of the spirit of the Gospel?

This is a vast question, which we shall be approaching only in circumscribed form: How, today, and using the liturgy laid down by Vatican II, can we avoid the veneer, collage, and degenerative practices described above, and foster the development of a living mode of practice which, being alive, will be evangelical and creative, and will both have roots in culture and root people in their culture?

To attempt to answer this question, we shall analyse various ways of looking at the celebration of the liturgy, and lay particular emphasis on the idea that seems to offer the best approach to developing a living practice of the liturgy, i.e., the idea of an operational model.

1. BASIC ANTHROPOLOGICAL STRUCTURES

It is well known that all symbolic activity is related to the human body, which itself is situated in the cosmos. Throughout the human race, the top and bottom, the right and left, the inside and outside of the body, and facing water, earth, wind or fire are 'figures' that enable man to speak—think—make the transexperimental world: life-death, heaven-hell, power-weakness, etc. The liturgy likewise is entirely structured by these bodily-cosmic figures: descent into—coming up from the waters of baptism; eating-and-drinking-together in the eucharistic meal; listening to—response to the Word; calling together—coming together—dispersal of assemblies, etc. We can never completely free ourselves of these figures. They affect every human being and are in a sense universal.

But we cannot deduce from this that a baptism or Eucharist will necessarily mean the same to everyone. Figures do not exist in the abstract; if they can be apprehended, they are already part of a culture. But cultures can obscure, distend, and even invert the meaning of the most basic anthropological structures. For many western Christians over a long period of time, the eucharistic bread was primarily there to be adored, not to be eaten. Even today, many people who attend an infant baptism think that the water washes away original sin. The deepest and most fundamental meanings are not necessarily the most obvious. Yet the aim of every reform is to restore them.

As we shall be saying later, much else besides basic anthropological structures will be needed if liturgy is to be Christian liturgy, that is, action charged with the significance of Christ. But in periods of cultural change like ours, with its reforms and innovations, it is very important that these basic structures be re-emphasised. There are two particular orthopractic principles which should be remembered:

(a) When one is brought to question forms of behaviour and interpretations from an earlier practice, for example relations within the group, modes of verbal communication, and the way respect is shown, one must be careful to note that some aspects of the liturgy are less open to change than others. There are some 'structuring' ways of patterning the celebration to overturn which is to run the risk of cutting oneself off from the sources of its meaning. Thus the main units of ritual (coming together—celebrating; listening—replying; bringing the food—sharing out—eating and drinking) contain an implicit logic which must be respected.

(b) When ritual behaviour becomes variable again, then unless there is spontaneous agreement about the significant forms, it is probably necessary for the competent authority to prescribe and explain them in order to get them accepted and understood. That is what happened with the recent reform. But as any mystagogue knows, prescribing and explaining are not the main point. They can come later. The first step should be to trust the power at work in the gestures that constitute the sacraments and not be afraid to try them in their complete form. If (adult) candidates for baptism are actually immersed, they will have a chance of seeing Romans 6 in its true light—and of being enlightened by it. If those who eat at the same eucharistic table really share the bread and the cup, they will understand John 6 and John 13 differently. If those who pray together actually raise their hands and prostrate themselves, the psalms will be able to come alive and speak to them. It is primarily by doing that that the believer will take root or take root anew. That is where the implantation of Christian worship starts. A beginning has already been made along these lines, but there is still a great deal to be done.

2. CONSTITUENT ELEMENTS

The natural world, artistic objects, historical documents and forms of human behaviour all may serve to ground a symbolic action. Christian liturgy chose selectivity from among them, giving special importance to traditional, biblical elements and those used in synagogues. Very early on, writers who mention Christian worship picked out regular and concordant material details: 'They come together on set days'; 'We have readings . . . and prayers'; 'Bread and wine are brought, and the person presiding gives thanks as best he can'. Thus a number of fixed details emerged and a tradition began to take shape.

Whenever reform, renewal and cultural adaptation have occurred, their purpose has been to 'decoke' and revitalise the elements which the Church recognises as constituting its liturgy. To take a well-known example, what is now called the 'Liturgy of the Word' is made up of Readings—Singing—Prayers. When the Instruction *Inter Œcumenici* laid down the principles for the Liturgy of Hours, it noted that four elements: Psalm—Hymn—Reading—Prayers were needed to constitute an 'Office'. Similarly when the eucharistic prayers for assemblies with children were being prepared, the group examining the proposals discussed the question: What are the essential elements which must occur in any eucharistic prayer?

But a liturgy is not just a collection of constituent elements, however essential. Their relative importance, the order in which they appear, and the way they are used still have to be decided.

Moreover, even when symbolic action is as complex as the liturgy, it needs more than the essentials if it is to work. Other things are always required to complete the sense of the action. (To take an analogy: a sentence does not only contain nouns and verbs, but connecting participles, verb endings, noun endings and tautologies, all of which determine the precise meaning.) Furthermore, history shows that liturgy always tends to let the essential elements become atrophied—witness the reduction of the responsorial psalm to one verse, in all rites, or singing obscuring the eucharistic prayer—and to expand the more recent adventitious elements which are seen as more expressive.

Reformers always proceed by returning to the essential elements and cutting back anachronistic growth. But they ought never to forget that the essential elements can only have value as symbols to the extent that they are grounded in the ambient culture. They can only be living symbols if they form part of the fabric of that culture. Otherwise they are just 'things' or 'ideas' unsuited to celebration.

3. PRESCRIBED RITUAL SCHEMES

It is impossible to establish when a rite or liturgy first came into being. We can only know them through successive states, each of which is a transformation of an earlier state. Our knowledge of these states is derived from descriptions of the kind: 'On such a day we go to such and such a place, in such and such order. So and so does such and such.

There is Bible-reading *x*. *y* is sung. Prayer *z* is said.' These descriptions are the origin of the Typica and Ordines, and later on of missals, breviaries and books of ritual. Originally, they were usually produced to give information about a particular pre-eminent liturgy that people elsewhere wanted to copy, e.g., the Armenians and Georgians with the Jerusalem liturgy, or the Franks with the Roman liturgy. But because any rite has an inherent tendency to become inflexible, the descriptions became increasingly normative, until the stage was reached where, before Vatican II, the Roman liturgy's definition of itself was 'what is "prescribed in the approved books" '.

Vatican II returned to the idea that liturgy is not a set of rubrics, but the essential activity of the Church at prayer. But the conciliar movement was trapped in the current western conception of liturgy as a set of rites laid down in detail and *ne varietur* for the universal (Roman!) Church. So when the reforms were undertaken, what else could it do but produce more books and more rubrics. This must surely have been the first time in history that a prescribed scheme of rites was the starting-point for renewed celebration of the liturgy. Previously, such collections had been descriptions or codifications of existing customs that were recognised as being good and normative, and even obligatory, within a specific human grouping. The manner of celebration had grown out of the custom and practice of the believing communities. But after Vatican II, liturgy appeared to be handed down from on high, through books written by experts and consisting mainly in prescribed ritual schemes.

True, there is a partial innovation, in that the books contain *General Introductions* or *praenotanda* which explain the spiritual meaning and pastoral import of the new rites. But it is questionable whether that alone can produce a living liturgy.

Celebrating and following a prescribed rite are two very different things, as attendance at some masses quickly shows. The rite may be followed accurately and faithfully, there may be obvious pastoral zeal, dignified singing, and a good homily, but the whole is cold and boring and no perceptible communication takes place. That is why many of the faithful now complain that 'Things are not what they used to be'.

Fortunately, the Vatican II books did not land in a vacuum: liturgy was already being enacted everywhere. When it was living prayer and there was the skill not to destroy but to transform, or when it was sluggish but reforms enabled it to be aroused, real 'celebration' continued. But the prescribed rite by itself would not have had the same result. It is only one element among many, and not always the most important.

4. OPERATIONAL MODELS

Celebration, festivity or ceremony becomes a collective symbolic activity when the group that is celebrating is engaged in a game with rules it knows well enough to find interesting and meaningful—lastingly so when an officially established celebration is involved. The question is: what is needed to make the game work, and work well?

(a) Preliminaries

First of all, the rules must be neither too flexible nor too rigid. We will illustrate this by describing two kinds of situation where they are too flexible, and two others where they are excessively strict.

When ritual was unshackled, after Vatican II, 'spontaneity' and 'creativity' became the vogue ideas. As a reaction against the preoccupation with rigid form and details of rubric that had gone before, there were demands for the liturgy to be an area of free expression, with no set schemes or ready-made formulae. Now there are indeed occasions when very homogeneous groups are capable of making up the rules of the game for themselves on the spur of the moment, at least to a certain extent. But in a group which is open to any believer of good will, as a Sunday assembly normally is, every habitual participant has to know what to expect, or else he will feel left out of the game. Moreover, it has often been noted that immediate spontaneity is usually superficial. True spontaneity comes from long familiarity. Lastly, so-called creativity opens the door to triteness and platitude. In ritual as in art, constraint is life and ease is death.

A second situation in which the rules may be too slack can occur when the participants are culturally unable to integrate with the rite, or, what amounts to the same thing, when the rite does not match their culture. In the case of isolated individuals, one sometimes has to allow for a quite normal period of initiation. But a whole community can be left untouched by the ceremonies because the rites have no symbolic basis in its daily life. Then there is a problem, which is in fact the problem to which the pastoral liturgical movement has been addressing itself in the twentieth century. It is that whereas the rules for officiating ministers were extremely strict, the rules for the faithful were so free that the faithful were hardly in the game at all. Vatican II, wanting to encourage active participation, attempted to resolve this problem. It did so within the framework of what was taken to be the present-day culture of Christians in the western world. Other parts of the world have had the door to cultural adaptation of the liturgy half-opened, but the machinery established has only just begun to be made use of.

In contrast with the two preceding situations, the rules may be so strict that the agent in charge of the celebration has not enough freedom of manoeuvre to make it live, or alternatively, only a few participants will be capable of playing the game in the manner expected, and a feeling of malaise will ensue.

It is not very long since officiating ministers of the Roman liturgy did no more than perform the prescribed rites, with absolutely no freedom to adapt them. And indeed, there was no reason to adapt them, when the faithful were expected neither to understand nor to participate. Vatican II altered the prescribed rites to fit 'the needs of our age' in order to get the faithful to take part. On some points ministers now have a degree of choice intended to let them make the service meet the needs of the assembly better. But as defined by the general law, and viewed in the light of experience, the area of free choice is extremely limited and totally inadequate.

While the clergy labour under the constraining requirement to conform to the established rites, the people for their part now have a quite different burden to bear. Think back for a moment how extraordinarily hospitable the Roman Latin liturgy of the last few centuries used to be. The only thing asked of people at mass was that they be there. They were not required to understand the texts and the symbols, or to demonstrate their solidarity, or to take part in the ordinary rites. The recent reform, which aims at the full, active, conscious and fruitful participation of the greatest possible number in the whole celebration has revealed how demanding liturgy is. There are the demands of Scripture in the vernacular, to be proclaimed (electronically amplified), and explained; the demands of the faith of the Church to be professed by all, and of prayers for today, often with highly 'committed' intentions; the demands of taking part in the singing, in styles that range from the archaic to the *avant-garde*; the demands of the sacrament of the Eucharist which of its nature implies communion. As a programme, an ideal, it is marvellous, and no one could fail to rejoice at it. But it assumes the existence of fervent and devout believers. Whereas in fact, in our assemblies, not everyone is capable of taking part in a game of this sort. And those who cannot play the game sometimes feel they do not belong, or even that they have been discarded.

(b) The Question

The question then is whether there is any way of running the celebration that can remain faithful to the substance of tradition but also enable the service to be adapted, as it needs to be, to the situation today, the assembly gathered together in the here and now, and its actual culture. Is there any mechanism that allows the best to penetrate as deeply as possible into the mystery but does not leave out the least of the poor, the uneducated or the misfits; that can take them by the hand and lead them along the way? If we take this as our aim, must we necessarily fall to one side or the other, and lapse into tense concentration on the rubrics or theological inflexibility, or else slip over into whimsicality and the cult of spontaneity?

As our examples will show, the way festivities, art and religious services function as social acts provide numerous point of reference to assist our reflection about the organisation of a 'successful celebration'. Between improvisation pure and simple, with its attendant risks of failure or superficiality, and total regulation, with its attendant dangers of boredom and lack of warmth, there is a third way, the re-play, which can draw on a wealth of memory but is open again to the grace of the moment, which has a stable basic pattern but is performed with freedom. This type of living re-play is both traditional and innovatory, and requires only of those who fill the main roles in celebrating the liturgy that they have the social competence and skill to apply the technique of what we are calling an 'operational model'.

(c) Examples

To guide us towards the operational model, let us take a few examples from different areas.

The Coptic eucharistic liturgy can last three hours on a feast-day, or one hour or less in an ordinary day. The liturgy itself is the same, and people accustomed to it can follow it easily. But the use of more melismatic or more syllabic chants, of more solemn or less solemn processions, of longer or shorter litanies, of prayers that can either be said quietly or be left out, and so on, allows the service to be extendable or compressible in time. It can vary also in its degree of festiveness.

An Eastern Orthodox cantor with a troparion to perform has one or more model melodies available, and adapts them to the text before him. As always with singers in an oral tradition, it is a known hymn that is sung, but no two performances of it are ever exactly the same; each performance is unique.

The men who sculpted the capitals of our cathedrals worked creatively from traditional 'models'. They used the same scenes and the same rules of execution and interpretation, but did not make 'copies'. Each artist adapted to the particular situation and retained his individuality.

Story-tellers provide another interesting example. The audience often knows the story already. Why then is it interested in hearing it again, since the teller changes neither the story, nor the sequence of episodes, nor the crucial passages everyone is waiting for, nor the fixed formulæ that are used? And yet he never tells the same story in the same way twice, and the listener's interest never flags.

A particularly illuminating example from our point of view concerns public prayer in the synagogues, according to patristic tradition. At the Sabbath 'blessings', the president was forbidden to 'read' the passage from a scroll. He had to begin with a silence, during which the participants said the prayer to themselves 'in their hearts'. During this time, the president had to think about how he was going to 'say' the prayer. He was therefore going to put into words a traditional prayer that everyone already knew by rote. But it would always sound as if it sprang from his heart then and there.

(d) The idea of the operational model

The operational model thus emerges as a form of symbolic behaviour which the celebrating group is familiar with, the participants have fully assimilated, and the main actors have adequately mastered. It allows the group to celebrate with peace of mind because the game and the rules are familiar. But it does not paralyse the action. Whatever is done is done as it were naturally and instinctively. The liturgy can emerge both as something remembered and as something new.

The operational model may be said to be the concrete form that the local way of Christian worship actually takes for a specific human group in a particular area at a given moment. Historically, it is approximately the equivalent of what liturgists call a 'rite'. For the western Syrian rite, the Byzantine rite and the Roman rite are surely just the various forms the liturgy assumed as it adapted and was adapted to the culture of a particular place and time. No living rite can be reduced to the mere description of its ritual scheme. Real knowledge of it depends on living it with the group.

(e) Applications

The operational model can be variously applied: to the celebration as a whole; or to its main units, the opening rites, the liturgy of the Word, and the eucharistic meal; or to individual rites such as a sung piece or a prayer. It enables the ceremony to be made lengthier on feast-days and shorter on ordinary days, something which has been difficult and uncommon since Vatican II because of the obligation to follow the prescribed ritual.

There are some sung rites which by their very nature call for the operational model technique. All those that require 'cantillation', musical or semi-chanting, come into this category. With prefaces, intoned pieces and introductions to prayers, which are normally performed solo, a 'written, literary' musical work can easily become irrelevant and turn into a concert piece. But the main danger is that the musical work can kill the 'living' word for performer and listener alike. Our western cultures need to start almost from scratch in this area. Fortunately, the requisite techniques are still in common practice in other parts of the world, such as Africa.

As for prayers by the president of the assembly, and the eucharistic prayer in particular, it is probably true to say that the only way to make them living moments of prayer by the Church here and now is to use the operational model. By its very nature, this prayer cannot be 'read' as one reads Scripture, a historical document. It is an action of the Church at the present moment. But it is also remembrance and a universal profession of faith. It has therefore to reconcile the traditional and the new in its very enactment—as what is called 'improvisation' doubtless did in the very early Christian liturgy.

Finally, the model allows even untalented ministers to be used without putting the service at risk. Since Vatican II the success or failure of services has too often been dependent on the personal qualities or weaknesses of the celebrants. But it is not their job to force the rite into existence; the rite itself, as a collective mode of behaviour, ought to enable ordinary members of the community to fill the various roles quite naturally.

(f) Reflections

The 'Roman rite' no longer exists as an operational model, except vestigially. The worshipping Christian communities in every cultural area of adequate size and vitality will have to encourage the resurrection of the operational models which are essential to easy, living and successful celebration of the liturgy. Much time and patience will be needed, for no one can create or invent a model. They are learnt and spread by being practised. But they also change continually in response to differing and sometimes contradictory influences, such as the prevailing secular taste or return to the sources, the prestige of a famous centre of worship, the influence of a well-known figure, or meeting other cultures and spiritualities; conversely they may become isolated and regress through lack of dynamism and external contact. Usually, a sound and healthy practice will develop its own roots in the local culture. When that happens, the rest can be left to the *sensus fidelium*, thanks to the Holy Spirit at work in all who pray and celebrate in the name of Jesus.

5. STYLE

It is the fact that there is an operational model that enables the same liturgy to be celebrated in a wide variety of styles. The *missa cantata* of the Roman rite I knew as a child was the same in the country parish where I was born, the nearby abbey of Solesmes and the cathedral of Angers. But the liturgy had a completely different style in each of the three places: the assembly, the singing and the ceremonies were distinctive and individual.

If a community is really to make the celebration its own, put it on and be at ease in it, it is quite natural that it should give it the individual and distinctive stamp of its own local style. The celebration then has flavour, like a local wine, a strong country accent or local folk art. And it has flavour for the local people as well as strangers.

The chance an operational model offers of giving the celebration a distinctive style and varying it according to the circumstances has a happy consequence: it lessens the need—which has become epidemic in some places—to be forever changing and updating formularies, sung repertories and even ritual schemes. This need came into existence when the Vatican II reforms were introduced, not just as a reaction against the earlier rigidity, but also because the liturgy generally become too hackneyed. When energies are directed solely to applying a prescribed set of rites which are theoretically uniform throughout the world and valid 365 days a year, the resulting liturgy will be in the image of our industrialised society with its mass-produced objects and reflect the so-called culture of the mass-media. If the life that can be provided by an operational model and the flavour that can come from a real style are missing, repetition of the same ritual elements soon makes them wear thin and leads to a desire for change. Then the endless race after a 'consumer' liturgy begins.

Any sensible beauty, as an authentic style reminds us, is individual and particular. And this individuation reflects the mystery of incarnation which extends via the order of symbol into the mysteries of the liturgy.

6. EXECUTION

Just as musical work exists only when it is performed at a particular time and place, by and for particular performers and listeners, in a production in sound that will always be unique, so a celebration of the liturgy is a unique event that happens on a particular day, for a particular assembly, in a particular place, with its own singing, its own preacher and its own socio-historical context (war or peace; social strife or harmony; an ordinary Sunday or a feast-day). Of it people will say: 'That was wonderful', or 'That was sad',—or not say anything at all. . . .

Liturgical symbols very often derive their greatest impact—both inherent and extrinsically induced—from the *kairos* of the actual celebration, not the way it is programmed. A word, a tune, a silence, an inflexion, a beam of light catching the wall suddenly 'speak'. The assembly feels an 'atmosphere', or individuals a 'grace'.

The importance of execution in liturgy is so obvious that to mention it may seem pure routine. But too often the liturgy of a place or part of the country one has been in once is judged good or bad simply because it was especially good or just plain bad that particular day. Furthermore, it is essential for ministers and the various people who play an active role to remember that, where communication is concerned, execution outweighs all other factors. The finest piece of music is liturgically bad if it is badly sung; the best piece is the simplest one, with which all can pray best. (That is not necessarily the musician's opinion.)

Lastly, the momentary and passing nature of any service and the ephemeral quality of any gathering destined to disperse should remind us that the mystery that has already been celebrated is followed by the hoped-for mystery yet to come. The eschatological nature of any liturgy is reflected in the fragile imperfection of all our celebrations.

Liturgical orthopraxis attempts to unite and hold in balance in the act of celebration the various aspects of liturgy we have been discussing: structuring anthropological figures, basic constituent elements, officially prescribed rites, the 'play' of operational model, colourful styles and meaningful execution.

But those who are in charge of the liturgy have limited power over the way it is celebrated. Symbols cannot be manipulated as if every rite ought to produce specific effects. In the order of symbol—a locus of creativeness and true history—the actual effects are for the most part unpredictable and unverifiable. The task of the pastor-liturgymaker is first to present the signs with forceful and ample dignity, and then to remove obstacles that may impede understanding of their sense and prevent the believer from freely situating himself with respect to them.

We will note just three of the general obstacles that have still to be overcome: (i) the passivity of assemblies that have not yet come to see that the celebration of the liturgy belongs to them, and is not the exclusive domain of a few ministers of religion; (ii) the heavy hand of the authorities who are still treating the prescribed rituals as total absolutes, so that it is difficult for assemblies to revive operational models and find their individual style; (iii) the zeal of liturgists who think they can imprison the way the liturgy is practised within their own idea of it, which is always too narrow and confined.

Thanks be to God, wherever there is the courage to celebrate in truth, tradition lives, the liturgy is taking root in culture, and there occurs the only creation that befits all liturgy: the coming, for and by the assembled believers, of the new world in the Risen Christ.

Translated by Ruth Murphy

Mary Collins

Obstacles to Liturgical Creativity

ANY ASSERTION that creativity is a central value for the Roman liturgy requires us to go beyond the terms on which the Roman Catholic Church currently understands its own liturgical tradition. The text of the Constitution on the Sacred Liturgy provides little overt support for the element of novelty which is at the heart of the theoretical analyses of creativity in the twentieth century. The conciliar document indeed authorised a series of transforming interventions relative to the liturgy: renewing, restoring, reinstating, returning, correcting, emending, altering, adapting, doing away with, setting aside, suppressing, even introducing and producing. But the very authorising of such interventions confirmed not simply the fact of a well-established tradition of public worship but also the responsibility of institutional authority to guard it. Not surprisingly, the official pronouncement on novelty was caution against it: there must be no innovations unless the good of the Church genuinely and certain requires them. Even when the good of the Church is at stake, any new form which might be adopted is expected to meet the criterion of growing organically from forms already existing (SC 23).[1]

Despite the magisterium's firm preference for the given rather than the novel, liturgiologists can point to many moments when bursts of liturgical creativity resulted in the displacing of the familiar by the unprecedented and in the gratuitous praise of God in novel but culturally congenial forms. The phenomenon of the continuing unselfconscious creativity of early generations of Christians, rediscovered in this century, has led one interpreter of the traditions to judge that the Church of the first eight centuries welcomed everything good and noble into the liturgy.[2]

The purpose of this essay is not to debate that matter, although it is debatable whether the Church consistently gained through its selective nurturing and suppressing of the unprecedented. The Chinese rites controversy is the most celebrated case, but it is not an isolated instance, nor necessarily the most important one, many women would argue. However, the essay is concerned with another matter. It aims first to establish a context for understanding present-day concern with liturgical creativity; next, to look at the creative process and the individual in the community as the agent of creativity; thirdly, to consider the social process by which the individual creative act enters the public tradition, and finally on the basis of these foundations to talk about the most serious obstacles to liturgical creativity in the Roman Catholic Church in this post-conciliar period.

1. CREATIVITY AS CULTURAL VALUE: TWO VIEWS

The notion that creativity is good and that a dearth of creativity is bad is relatively recent even in western culture. Talk of human creativity first appeared relative to the individual artist as late as the nineteenth century and was extended to other human enterprise like economics, city planning, and liturgical worship only in the twentieth. Prior to this, God alone was called creator, since the concept creation meant fashioning something from nothing. In the nineteenth century, however, creation came also to mean making something new, and those able to generate the novel were called creative. The esteem for human creativity has grown steadily in western culture, leading one philosopher to note that an indifferent or negative attitude towards creativity is virtually incomprehensible to contemporary people. It is in this cultural context that efforts to promote or inhibit liturgical creativity are taking place. Not surprisingly, the 'ideology of creativity' has itself come under critical scrutiny recently.[3]

Some say western preoccupation with human creativity simply mirrors the consumer culture and its taste for the novel, or the technological mentality for which the manufacture of a new product is good in itself. It is also said that the willingness to cherish individual self-expression as the supreme value of life is a natural outcome of this exaltation of creativity. The 'punk' decadence of western European youth is thought to be intelligible within this perspective. Such themes provide the basis for most negative judgments on the late twentieth century western preoccupation with creativity.

But another more benign interpretation is possible. Creativity may be a 'category of difficult life' according to an observer who notes that the fascination with human creativity and individual self-expression has paralleled the rise of the totalitarian state and the post-industrial mass society.[4] People who promote 'creativity' are doing so, in this view, because of the conditions of their social existence, namely, life lived under institutions which diminish or curtail the human spirit. Exaltation of creativity in such situations might best be heard as the longing of peoples for transcendence and for the transformation of dehumanising social forms. Considered on these terms, it is possible to look positively on the recent western preoccupation with creativity.

This philosophical discussion bears on efforts to understand developments relative to the Roman liturgy since Vatican II. In one form or another, each of these themes has appeared during the last fifteen years in the pages of *Notitiae*, the official publication of the Congregation for Divine Worship. The negative motif has been sounded recurrently to curb the perceived taste for novelty on the part of the clergy. Warnings seem to rise from and to be directed primarily to established churches in the North Atlantic countries, the cultural homeland of individualism. On the other hand, *Notitiae* has also published in its pages the liturgical programme of the bishops heading the churches of the poor in Latin America. These churchmen assert that their peoples must have new forms for public worship precisely because so many lives are intolerably miserable. In order for these poor to be empowered to collaborate with Christian hope to overcome the political, economic, and social forces that oppress them, their bishops say that the worshipping assembly must itself be open to the liturgically unprecedented. Here the positive judgment prevails: creativity is a 'category of difficult life'.

Notitiae also reflects a positive Roman attitude towards the introduction of the unprecedented in the liturgical forms of the young churches of Africa and the minority churches of Asia. The welcome of the novel into the liturgical assemblies clearly aims to affirm the human spirit manifested in the cultural ethos of these non-western peoples. Yet the very ambivalence of official Roman response to the post-conciliar impetus towards liturgical creativity invites further reflection.[5] Is novelty tolerable, permissible, desirable? For some but not all churches in the Roman rite? What are adequate criteria for making a positive or negative judgment on the creative impulses of local churches? Where is individualism at work? Where the effort to overcome human diminishment through celebration of the reign of God?

When philosophers evaluate the public significance of new art works and new social arrangements they focus on a central point: what is the impact of this novelty on the human community? Will the novel element generated by someone's unprecedented response to life help to build up the common tradition? Does it consolidate group identity and loyalty in changing times? Does it enable people to move forward together in a new situation? Does it break the power of repressive forces that constrict human hearts? Or does the novelty fragment the community? Does it increase alienation and group instability by encouraging individualism? Any of these outcomes is possible with the introduction of novelty into the public world of meaning. Underlying all the questions are a pair of clear criteria: is the new element intelligible to the community? and is it valuable for its life?[6]

2. CREATIVITY: THE PERSONAL ACT WITHIN A COMMUNITY

The novel element initially appears in the world of private imagination because someone searching for meaning perceives it as both intelligible and valuable. Imaginative individuals within a social group are the original locus of any form of creativity, whether artistic, social, or liturgical. In imaginative women and men the common tradition of public meanings meets the expansive human spirit aspiring to be and to understand more, and a creative interchange occurs.

Inculturation theory suggests that religious and so liturgical creativity is likely to occur as a local community with a generally coherent cultural system of public meanings, symbols, and behaviours seeks to appropriate to itself in culturally congenial forms the living tradition of Gospel faith which is already embodied in the cultural forms of earlier generations of believers.[7] Two currents converge to create a new one. But the creativity leading to that convergence begins inevitably in the private realm, and the agents of genuine creativity are seldom those who exercise authority over either operative tradition or conscious public meanings, ecclesial or civil. The genuinely creative form rises from the unconscious, and most predictably from persons searching for new possibilities of meaning not yet available in either tradition. Inculturation theory presupposes sparks of creative imagination already glowing in a community.

But imaginative persons venture more than their less imaginative sisters and brothers. They entertain images whose integration is possible only at the cost of the destabilisation or even the disruption of the known symbolic world. If the entertainment of unfamiliar images from private visions should yield new intelligibility, imaginative persons are often willing and at times even compelled to express publicly what they see. They will rearrange and even recreate the symbolic world for the sake of personal integration of their own further insight. Imaginative persons become creative, producing the unprecedented as they work at the psychic integration which generates insight and augments meaning for them personally.

Still, more than personal integration may be achieved. Once the novel has become known in the cultural community, it may eventually be welcomed into the common public tradition. Inculturation theory becomes pertinent here. So does other research into processes of social endorsement.[8] Development within the public tradition depends on the community's readiness, leaders and members alike, to affirm that the new symbol or form is both intelligible and valuable. The community of faith is the sole arbiter of what religious creativity it will receive from its own members and employ publicly in its common life.

The dynamic of what is now being called inculturation can be recognised in the well-known achievements of those liturgically creative fourth-century churches within which bishops like Cyril, Ambrose, Theodore, and John Chrysostom presided. The communities these men served in the Mediterranean basin shared in common pre-Christian Hellenistic and Roman cultural strains that were the result of past military conquests. In addition, each population centre also had the residual cultural features of pre-imperial indigenous local populations. Since every cultural tradition is a complex expression of true but only partial achievements of human community and meaning, each was open to new expressions of the human spirit.

Cultures are porous. Imaginative people, who lack the longevity of either culture or institutions, are ironically the pores of both. What gains entrance at a human point of permeability may eventually transform both the social community and the system of symbols by which it coheres. The Mediterranean cultures are an obvious historical illustration of this process which was operating long before the Gospel of Christ was proclaimed as a way of life. However, during the fourth century when the Gospel of Jesus Christ which had first seeped quietly into the low spots of imperial culture entered full-flood into the mainstream of public life, the creative interchanges and the new integrations which resulted had profound consequences. Nothing was the same: not the cultures, not the rites for public worship, not the peoples who came to the assemblies where the great bishops presided, nor the bishops themselves.

Yet what subsequent generations of Christians know about the creativity of these churches is what was finally integrated into its common life and its liturgical assemblies. It is unlikely that what became part of the recorded tradition exhausts the range of what was conceived and even tried by imaginative believers in the effort to express what faith in the Gospel of Jesus Christ meant in the fourth-century communities. What was finally overlooked or set aside was not necessarily false or worthless. It is at least likely that at times a church closed its eyes to the blinding insight of one of its gifted members, opting for a less painful light. Creative individuals offer their gifts. Whether and why and how these are received touches on another set of social dynamics. What is perceived as confusing or dangerous will not gain entrance.

3. INSTITUTIONAL SANCTION OF CREATIVITY

The 1963 Constitution on the Sacred Liturgy discloses the current formal arrangement by which any ritual creativity relative to the Roman liturgy must receive a triple warrant, at the local, national or regional, and Roman or central levels (SC 40). The arrangement reflects a practical judgment about suitable means to maintain the community of faith in the praise of God and the sanctification of diverse peoples. Even the most stable human institutions, the Church among them, must have mechanisms for enabling creativity to effect institutional change or for inhibiting such an outcome. Someone must be authorised to apply the twin criteria of intelligibility ('the new form must grow organically from forms already existing') and value ('the good of the Church is at stake') to the liturgically novel.

Before any formal judgment occurs at the institutional centre, many informal judgments take place at its margins. The creative person communicates the gift of new form or new meaning, a personal achievement but by no means yet a public one. Others in the community must begin to entertain the creative gift with its correlative gain into the meaning of the life of faith. Aesthetic concerns are not insignificant in the initial presentation of the new form or meaning, but they are seldom decisive. In fact the creative individual will begin to recede in importance as the gift is entertained.[9] Does this attempt to reorder the world of common public meaning allow the community to see and to absorb a new vision and yet to keep a firm grasp on the common tradition? The community will inevitably suffer a measure of destabilisation as it is confronted with the unfamiliar. But if the new insight originally born through the individual psyche's creative achievement has power to reveal meaning latent in the tradition, it will stimulate emotional, intellectual, aesthetic and moral response from others within the community. As that broadened base of response signals a valuable augmentation of the tradition, others will take it up, even promote it, and the social group will have moved a step closer to sanctioning the gain as a public achievement.

The formal sanctioning of the novel requires endorsement of the official authorities in the community, those who are vested with responsibility to 'guard the tradition'. Two human factors can impede this step. One is the private preference or personal sensibilities of the official judges, which leads them to respond indifferently to one possibility, enthusiastically to another, and with suspicion towards a third. The second factor is the tendency of those who hold the common tradition in trust to identify its interests with their own, so that what threatens personal or group interests is perceived to threaten the tradition. In this situation, the gift of form and meaning offered by the creative member and welcomed in the community may be significantly modified by the endorser, if it is endorsed at all, to weaken its impact on the public life of the community and so to protect those vested interests.

Recognition of these two obvious obstacles at the level of official judgment opens up the more complex question of authenticity or inauthenticity in the whole Church's response to the liturgically unprecedented. The fact of the existence of parish, diocesan, national, regional, and Roman liturgical authorities does not guarantee that judgments rendered at each level will always work to the good of the Church. Group inauthenticity is a factor to be dealt with in any discussion of the dynamics of liturgical creativity. It can operate at every level, posing the most serious obstacle to lively and life-giving gains in the forms of public worship.

4. OBSTACLES TO DESIRABLE INNOVATION

Earlier it was noted that a community will resist new forms and meanings which are confusing or dangerous; the ecclesial community is no exception. But not all novelty has such consequences. For example, much of the liturgically unprecedented which the bishops of Latin America, Asia, and Africa are calling for is that novelty of liturgical form which will allow a people to express its praise of God in the many languages of its own culture: its rhythms, its colours, its code of social decorum and hospitality, its dress, its ecological harmony with its own environment. These elements introduced into the liturgy will serve to bond the people to the Roman Catholic Church. Such developments will not endanger a people's sense of well-being, nor do they threaten to impinge on the well-being of the rest of the Church, unless, of course, a worshipping community lives with the notion that worship has to do with disengagement from life. Normally such changes are easily judged to be intelligible. But are they the only valuable kind of innovation?

A theological consideration must be introduced. All liturgy is the Church's symbolic enactment of the mystery of Christ and the Church. It is theologically sound to celebrate the mystery of salvation using forms which assert the dawning reign of God in human history in all its particularity. But a peculiar creativity, that of the Christian believer, is required to maintain evangelical tension within liturgical assemblies so that they are not merely mimetic of human achievement but a manifestation of what more the reign of God promises (SC 2). Because the irruption of the reign of God in history is dangerous, genuine liturgical creativity cannot help but be potentially so.

Accordingly, it is not only possible but probable that certain liturgical innovations which some see as confusing or dangerous are also both valuable and intelligible for the advancement of the Gospel at the end of the twentieth century. But to be open to their value and meaning demands conversion. Yet as the Canadian theologian Bernard Lonergan notes in his discussion of individual and group bias, certain insights are unwanted because they lead to correction and revision.[10] A Church which prefers to repent and believe the good news selectively will protect itself from dangerous insights operative in some forms of liturgical innovation, favouring the harmless. Three strategies are readily available to obstruct what is unwanted. They have to do with appeals to doctrinal orthodoxy, to power, and to human traditions.

Resistance to innovations with regard to liturgical ministers in the face of evident need is symptomatic of radical resistance to dangerous inbreaking of the Spirit of Jesus even in the Church. New arrangements for liturgical ministry, once authorised, will undermine the past achievement of ecclesial order and the theology which supports it, leading to an unknown future.[11] What kind of Church will it be in which the pastoral care and anointing of the sick, the witnessing and blessing of Christian marriages, the reconciliation of sinners, the celebration of the Eucharist, and the formation of new Christians are recognised as the right and responsibility of the whole community of the baptised? But what kind of a Church is it which fails to heal, strengthen, and nourish, to preach the Gospel, to bless, and to give thanks together because of a shortage of seminary-trained ordinands? What corrections and revisions in self-understanding will be demanded of the laity, of presbyters and deacons, of bishops, of the bishop of Rome, as these ecclesial constituents seek to open themselves to the value and truth of new possibility in the liturgical celebration of the mystery of Christ at work in the world? It is in the immediate interest of many to resist further innovation in liturgical ministry. It is not so clear that it is in the interest of fidelity to the apostolic mission of the Church. Nevertheless, theological arguments can easily be joined to impede the development of liturgical ministries, forming in the name of doctrinal orthodoxy a screen against the creative insights rising in worshipping communities in every country. Liturgical innovation will require theological reinterpretation.

If theological obscurantism is one likely impediment to liturgical innovation, the high-handed use of institutional power is another. A single example will illustrate. In the 1970s growing numbers of liturgical assemblies in North America hospitably received the use of flat bread baked by a member of the assembly in occasional and even Sunday Eucharists. Diocesan liturgical commissions monitored the practice quietly; the Canadian episcopal commission studied the matter theologically, historically, even scientifically. It prepared to release guidelines to shepherd the development, seeing in it a legitimate effort to assure that the bread of the Eucharist was a convincing bread-sign, as required by the 1970 *Ordo Missae* (283). Roman curial intervention aborted the work of local and national commissions. Roman Catholic eucharistic assemblies in North America still remain hospitable to the notion that the specialness of the bread of the Eucharist demands that it not be the product of assembly line host-making technology but the evident work of human hands, bread to be broken and shared as a pledge of commitment to discipleship. So the practice persists, somewhat less widespread now. However, bishops are not allowed to guide it nor to develop catechesis to interpret it; the Roman congregation expect bishops merely to suppress it.

High-handed uses of institutional power point to the delicate balance which must be maintained in the liturgical phase of the inculturation process. Inculturation theory asserts that the agents of creative appropriation of the received tradition to a cultural community are the community's own members, not those who represent the tradition's earlier achievements.[12] Where the balance of ecclesial authority—diocesan, national, and central—is not held in tension, liturgical innovations which are both intelligible and valuable will continue to be snatched abruptly from worshipping communities.

Episcopal authenticity requires that bishops claim their pastoral responsibility and reintroduce tension into the balance of institutional power. Evangelical authenticity requires that worshipping communities press their claim for worship forms which give expression to life-giving insights into the dawning reign of God which is present, proclaimed, and celebrated in the liturgy.

Unfortunately, low levels of energy and commitment in worshipping communities harbour the third major obstacle to significant liturgical innovation. Significance implies that the unprecedented forms with their correlative insights reveal to the Church more intimately and more powerfully the living Christ present and available for the world's reconciliation, for its conversion as well as its comfort. Each culture where the Church dwells participates in a distinctive way in the social disorder which manifests the sin of the world. The Christian liturgical assembly which fails to reveal the reconciling power of the reign of God is a flaccid manifestation instead of a dying Body of Christ. Such assemblies abound. In Mexico City on the feast of Our Lady of Guadalupe the powerful ecclesiastical and civil élites gather inside the basilica with US tourists to eat the eucharistic table. Outside, thousands of peasants remain marginalised even on this patronal feast, performing ritual dances in the square to memorialise the coming of the Spanish conquistadores who shaped their world and diminished their humanity. There is no hint in either of these assemblies that anyone present believes in the power of baptism and the Church's Eucharist to overcome this division.

Human sinfulness generates institutions which use human differentiation as the basis for the aggrandisement of some persons at the cost of the diminishment of others. Anyone can see each 12 December in Mexico City unredeemed racism wearing the aura of sacred celebration, and no diocesan or national or central authority nor the people itself says 'blasphemy' and requires authentic liturgy in the name of Christ. But one can find virtually everywhere liturgical assemblies which do the same thing, honour human arrangements that separate races, tribes, castes, classes, and the sexes, and mindlessly do so without reference to the mission and ministry of Christ and his Church.

The shaping of new liturgical forms to affirm the value and dignity of each people is one level of the challenge for liturgical creativity. The reshaping of familiar forms to reveal the power of Christ to overcome actual human disorder and establish the reign of God is another. These must both happen if liturgical creativity is an expression of ecclesial authenticity. The second dimension will undoubtedly be experienced as confusing and dangerous in apparently prosperous ecclesial communities. These can take up in their defence theological obscurantism, high-handed uses of institutional power, spiritual and aesthetic delight in the familiar. Churches poorer in such resources because of a searching faith may be the weak point where the Spirit of Jesus will break through, giving an almost impervious Church new ritual forms, new insight, and newness of life it does not yet find intelligible or valuable.

Notes

1. *Sacrosanctum Concilium* 23. Subsequent references will be noted only in the text.
2. K. Seasoltz *New Liturgy, New Law* (Collegeville 1980) p. 184.
3. Pertinent papers delivered at an international conference on Creativity and Social Life held at Jablonna, Poland in August 1978, are published in *Dialectics and Humanism* 4 (1977) and 5 (1978).
4. B. Suchodolski 'Creativity-Reality: Hopes and Doubts' *Dialectics and Humanism* 5 (1978) 29ff.

C

5. See volumes 5, 7, 13, 18 for examples of positive response to innovation; see volumes 8, 13, 14, 15 for typical warnings.

6. C. Hausman 'Criteria of Creativity' *Philosophy and Phenomenological Research* 40 (1979) 237-249.

7. A. Roest Crollius 'What Is So New About Inculturation?: A Concept and Its Implications' *Gregorianum* 59 (1978) 735.

8. See R. Firth 'Private Symbols and Public Reaction' in *Symbols: Public and Private* (Ithaca and London 1973) pp. 207-240.

9. The work cited in note 8, at pp. 230-240 provides foundations for this discussion.

10. B. Lonergan *Insight* (San Francisco 1957); see pp. 187-193.

11. M. Collins 'The Public Language of Liturgy' *The Jurist* 41 (1981) 261-294.

12. A. Roest Crollius, in the article cited in note 7, 733.

PART II

Historical Investigations

Pedro Farnes Scherer

Creative Improvisation, Oral and Written, in the First Centuries of the Church

1. PRELIMINARY CONSIDERATIONS

(a) Subject and Approach

THERE IS a wide preoccupation today, particularly in Catholic circles, with the subject of creativity and improvisation in liturgical matters. There are not a few who would argue that Vatican II opened up new possibilities in this respect which have since been unfulfilled. Some would hold as incontrovertible the fact that liturgical improvisation, as understood today, was a regular practice in the early Church and that a return to this practice would therefore show greater fidelity to the spirit of the Gospel. In support of this thesis, they point to eminent historians of the liturgy who, at least at first sight, seem to lend weight to this argument.[1] For this reason, careful analysis of the subject in order to discover what really was the practice of the early Church is required, and even urgent.

This study proposes to take a few of the most significant elements from the liturgy of the first centuries of the Church—there is obviously not space for an exhaustive catalogue—and situate them in their historical and existential context. The documents from the early days are well known today, so this study cannot hope to add anything startlingly new in the way of proof of their creativity or traditionalism. What might be more original is the second aspect of the approach: seeing how far particular expressions meant the same thing in their time as they are understood to mean today. If their real meaning is not quite what it seems to be at first glance, this can afford us an interesting insight into what the liturgical celebrations of the early Church were actually like.

Moving on from the significance of the history of early sources for liturgical theology and practice today, I think it important to stress one aspect that is not always given its due weight: the principle that in the field of liturgical theology—as in other fields of theology—there is or can be real progress in the sense that it is not always the most ancient forms that best express the Christian mystery, nor do modern developments always mean a falling away from the best. While such progress may not be possible with regard to actual Christian Revelation (since what is from God cannot be improved upon)—in our case the basic content of the celebration handed on by our Lord himself—there can still be real progress in the manner in which this revealed content is

29

expressed and embodied. So it is quite possible for a liturgical usage of the twentieth century to be more expressive of the Christian mystery than some of the early usages.[2] To move, for example, from liturgical formulations that in the beginning were somewhat fluid—though not to the extent of being 'creative improvisation', since this never actually existed, as we shall see—to more uniform and established formulations can in itself represent either progress or deterioration in fidelity to the Gospel message. Such progress or deterioration does not in any way depend exclusively on whether the liturgical expressions used are rigidly fixed or somewhat flexible, but mainly on the objective content of each of the formularies used and their meaning in the context of the liturgical act.

(b) Defining the terms

In Scholastic times, theologians and philosophers used to head their treatises with what was known as an *explicatio terminorum*. This facilitated dialogue between different parties by ensuring that the discussion itself did not degenerate into a mere semantic argument. This practice is not so general today, but here I think it is not only advisable, but even necessary, the reason being that there is such a wide gamut of possible meanings attached to terms such as 'creativity' and 'improvisation'—a few decades ago, Taylor could distinguish more than a hundred meanings of the word 'creativity'[3]—that it is easy to hide completely different realities under the cloak of the same terms and so not know precisely what is under discussion when we talk about 'creative improvisation'.

There is another reason for beginning with a careful definition of the term 'creative improvisation'. This is the fact that today all Christian communities tend to give the concept of creativity in liturgy such an affective charge that they sometimes endanger the historical accuracy of the meaning they attach to the sources, and with this the objectivity of the arguments with which they support one thesis or another. What generally happens, in fact, is that 'creativity' and 'improvisation' become virtually synonymous with 'progress', 'freedom', 'the spirit of the Council', while the use of previously established formulations comes to be 'inward-looking', 'authoritarian', 'routine', showing a 'pre-conciliar' or even 'anti-conciliar' mentality. A little reflection will show that starting with preconceptions of this sort and giving them—without any critical thought whatsoever—the value of principles, is hardly likely to lead to objectively valid conclusions. Hence the extra need to be careful about defining terms at the outset, since it is only in the light of a careful definition that we can go on to reflect on the true significance of the documents bequeathed to us by history.

One need really look no further than the title of this article (given to me, not my choice!) to see what I mean. It can be somewhat ambiguous, since the juxtaposition of the adjective 'creative' and the noun 'improvisation' seems to suggest that both qualities generally went together, whereas in fact they were just as often separated, since we are dealing with two concepts that differ by their nature from one another. 'Creative' really suggests that there was nothing there before, and the Council was very selective in its use of the term. The concept of 'creativity' does not appear at all in the Constitution on the Sacred Liturgy: in fact it appears only twice in all the conciliar documents, both times in *Gaudium et Spes*, once in the strict philosophical sense referring to the creative activity of God,[4] and once in an analogous sense applied to the activity of modern man who through the application of his intelligence can be said to 'create' by introducing '*profound* and rapid changes'.[5] In the liturgical sphere, however, the term creativity would be less appropriate than 'adaptation' since we are not dealing with 'profound' changes in the basic part of the celebration handed down by our Lord but rather of adaptations in the manner of celebrating, designed to reconcile the eternal truths to the mentality of people today. And so it is precisely this word, adaptation, that the Constitution on the Liturgy uses.[6]

(c) The meaning of 'creative improvisation'

Expressions such as 'improvisation' and 'creativity' are in general use today, but not everyone attaches the same meaning to them. So let us examine the phrase 'creative improvisation', which is what we have then to search the early texts for. To improvise means 'to compose, utter, extempore' (COD), 'to compose (verse, music, etc.) on the spur of the moment' (WED). Larousse backs this up for French: '*composer sur le champ*', and in Spanish the Academy Dictionary gives first the general meaning of 'doing something on the spot, without any previous study or preparation'. Turning to 'creative', COD gives the first meaning of 'to create' as 'to bring something into existence', implying that it did not exist before. Larousse is more explicit, with '*tirer du néant*', and the Spanish Academy has 'to produce something from nothing'. These definitions all have an ancient basis: St Thomas in his *Summa theologica* defines creating as 'making something out of nothing'.

So if we put the two together, we are bound to conclude that the phrase 'creative improvisation' should be used strictly as meaning the composition of something totally new, based not on existing texts or ideas, but on 'nothing', and, furthermore, doing this 'extempore', '*sur le champ*', without 'previous study or preparation'. So any such 'creative improvisation' would have to imply a distancing from anything that could be considered previous usage, tradition. If this is what the expression means . . . we can say that no such phenomenon was known in the early Church. If the meaning of 'to improvise' is extended to include the *intention* of doing something without study or preparation . . . then perhaps its champions will begin to think twice about defending it.

However, the exact semantics are one thing. Another is the sense in which the expression is used by those who defend total flexibility of liturgical forms of worship. An examination of the collections of Collects, Anaphoras, Bidding Prayers, etc., proposed by the defenders of free creativity in liturgy will show that the authors' ideal is nearly always the greatest novelty of text, truly new and original, and as far removed as possible from the 'official' prayers of the Church.

(d) Other possible forms of liturgical flexibility

If this is what is understood by 'creative', both in the strict linguistic sense and in general usage by the proponents of 'creativity' in liturgy, we need not think that its opposite has to be absolute rigidity. A brief look at two other possible forms of flexibility in liturgy should help both to elucidate early practice and to suggest ways of giving fresh vitality to our services today. This will show to what extent certain expressions in the early documents refer to actual improvisation in forms of worship or only to a certain degree of flexibility. This is basic both to a correct historical understanding of the early texts and to an understanding of the main lines of later liturgical interpretation, which has in fact been faithful to early practice, if not always in practice, then at least in spirit.

The first form of flexibility other than 'creative improvisation' is *adaptation* of existing formulations. And as we have seen, the Constitution on the Liturgy gives ample space to the idea of adaptation, while not mentioning the concept of 'creativity'.[7] Post-conciliar liturgical reform also uses the term more than once.[8] Such an adaptation, far from 'making something out of nothing', consists in modifying existing liturgical expressions—either in their literary form or even in some minor aspects of their actual content—so as to make them more intelligible or authentic in relation to a particular assembly of worshippers. There are obviously endless applications of this form of adaptation. It is a process that has nearly always gone on and one required by the very concept of truth in prayer. It lapsed only in times of outstanding liturgical decadence and its disappearance was obviously linked to incomprehension of liturgical language. The more lively and popular liturgy is at any time, the more the practice of adaptation of its formulations will be in evidence. It is this sort of adaptation, I would suggest, that the famous text of Hippolytus which we shall examine later has in mind,[9] and the new liturgical books also refer to it frequently.[10] It can be written or even improvised; it depends not so much on predetermined attitudes (it is better to 'adapt' as one goes; 'changes' should be prepared beforehand) as on the very nature of the adaptations made. The Directory for Masses for Children would seem to require that adaptations be normally written; on the other hand, to adapt the plural expression 'we your servants, and all your holy people' in the Roman canon to the singular 'I your servant . . .' when only one minister is presiding, is something that can easily be improvised by paying attention to the meaning of the words. The same is true of the adaptations proposed by the *Missale Romanum* for the euchological texts in masses for the dead.[11]

The second form of liturgical flexibility is the *composition of new texts*. This form is obviously more attractive to those who want to see a liturgical celebration with a more modern accent and more firmly rooted in the realities of the day. This possibility is distinguished from 'creative improvisation' in that it is carefully prepared and, if carried out according to the wishes of Vatican II, is certainly not done 'from nothing', but takes its inspiration from traditional euchology, incorporating new present-day realities if you like, but not throwing out the old for the sake of the new. This composition of new texts, while more attractive, is also more dangerous in some ways—not least in that the compositions of recent times can 'date' much more quickly than those of ancient times: one only has to think of the pietistic nature of nineteenth-century masses for newly canonised saints.

Again, this is a process that has always gone on in the Church, though less at some times than at others. It was clearly most common in the foundational period: the birth of texts for worship had to accompany the birth of the Church. Among these the most important has to be the New Testament itself (though it was not the first in time), as much of it was composed for use in worship.[12] It is not the most ancient liturgical text because, as modern biblical studies show ever more clearly, it includes many passages which were widespread through liturgical use before they were written down in what became the New Testament.[13] After the foundational period, new texts for the liturgy have been composed continually, from the *Didache* and the *Apostolic Tradition* of Hippolytus in the first to third centuries, to the new compositions approved after Vatican II, through those composed in the middle ages and not excluding even the liturgically most decadent centuries, in which each new saint canonised and each new devotion approved meant new liturgical texts composed according to the taste of the period. At some periods, there was such an abundance of new texts being composed that we today might well wonder at the amount of activity going on in what we might regard as a period of liturgical decadence.[14] And in our own day, with the general reform of the Liturgy decreed by Vatican II,[15] it is not surprising that there should be a volume of composition of new texts if not equal to, then not far behind, that of the early period when the various rites of the Christian liturgy were first taking shape. This situation is a new stimulus to study of the experience of the early Church, to see how far the earliest communities improvised, adapted or composed the texts used in their celebrations. So let us now take a look at the early texts and what they might mean.

2. THE TEXTS AND WHAT THEY MEAN

(a) How to present and interpret the texts

So far we have examined the meaning of expressions such as 'creativity', 'improvisation', 'adaptation' and 'composition of new texts' in the field of liturgical euchology. Establishing their meaning helps to tackle the texts that have come down to us from the early days of the Church with greater ease and exactitude. These texts are many and are beginning to become more widely known so rather than list them—for which there is anyway no space here—I propose to take some of the most significant facts they relate and some of the more interesting phrases they contain and place them in their historical context. This is the only way to discover what a particular phrase might have meant at the moment when it was written. Things written at a great distance from us in time and cultural context should not be interpreted anachronistically as though they had been written by our contemporaries. We have to try to go beyond the words used to find out what they really meant at the time when they were written. This is not easy, and some of my interpretations may well be open to question, but if they can serve to open a discussion on a subject which, in my view, has only been dealt with on the basis of over-literal interpretations, without taking a whole range of related facts into account, they will have served their purpose.

The best way, it seems to me, of reaching a correct understanding of these texts is to correlate the expressions they use with other writings or events of the time, or, failing that, of the time as near as possible to them. So if, for example, we come across an expression whose apparently obvious meaning refers to something we know did not exist at the time, we at least have to question whether that interpretation is correct. There might be a different reality veiled under the same set of words.

(b) Jewish sources of Christian liturgy

Studies carried out in the last few decades have shown increasingly clearly that there was a very close relationship between Jewish liturgy—that of the synagogue and of the various family services—and Christian liturgical writings. This fact, of which enough has perhaps not been made when considering the freedom of Christian liturgical formulations, is of the greatest importance here since it shows beyond doubt that, from the very foundation of the Church, we are dealing with *adaptation* rather than *creativity*, even taking the latter in the broad sense of merely composing more or less original prayers. Furthermore, this relationship between Jewish texts and Christian formulae is not a sporadic one limited to particular communities but rather the backdrop common to all the early liturgies we know. This fact forces us to recognise that the first Christian communities did not organise their ceremonies on the basis of which might occur spontaneously to anyone who happend to preside—even though some *isolated* texts might give this impression[16]—but following formulas that, at least in their main lines, were very fixed and traditional. (In this respect, studies by Botte in the history of philology and Daniélou in the history of theology are very significant and throw a lot of light on the matter.)

Accepting the interdependence between Jewish liturgy and early Christian liturgy, we should (briefly) note another important point: the fact that Israel in its liturgy was a long way from what we think of today as 'creative improvisation'. Despite the fact that the Jewish rabbi did not have a text in front of him when directing the liturgy of his community, he was not improvising the prayers. To think he was would certainly be anachronistic. If the president of the assembly did not read the prayers this was mainly because the culture of the time was above all an oral tradition. Written texts were always few and far between and so more reliance was placed on memory than on writing. The texts of the Bible themselves followed this route of being memorised long before being written down. That great student of Israelite liturgy, Hruby, declares roundly that: 'variants found in the texts of the prayers are relatively minor and hardly ever affect their content'.[17] Dealing with prayers for feast-days, for example, the *Mishna* states that the rabbi should familiarise himself with the *traditional* manner of making the prayer.[18] One particularly clear example of how this conservative mentality went from the worship of Israel to that of the Church is provided in Book VIII of the *Apostolic Constitutions:* right into the fourth century, the Christian community *conserved*, with only minor re-touches, an ancient Jewish ritual from the synagogal office for the Sabbath with its original prayers and formulas.

(c) The New Testament writings

Exegetes today are generally agreed that before they came to figure in the biblical text many passages of the New Testament were liturgical units—ritual descriptions or euchological pieces—which only came to be regarded as belonging to the Gospels or other apostolic writings through their repeated use in liturgical celebrations. This is true, for example, of the account of the Last Supper, of the multiplication of the loaves, of the final verses of Matthew with the trinitarian baptismal formula, and of the hymnic fragments in the letters of the Apostles or the Apocalypse. This is a new and important element which also shows how the Christian liturgy felt itself *tied* to traditional and apostolic formulas and usages.

(d) Early evidence for a certain liturgical rigidity

Let us now look at some particularly important pieces of evidence, first those that seem to suggest continuity in relation to the conservative atmosphere we find in Jewish sources and the New Testament itself; then some that seem to suggest the opposite, stressing rather freedom and even improvisation in the early Christian liturgy.

The earliest evidence we possess for the establishment of texts is the *Didache*. This document, which might be called 'the oldest Christian ritual', prompts the following observations: (i) its undeniable Judaeo-Christian character again confirms that the early Christians did not 'create' in liturgy, but always adapted: (ii) its numerous written and well-established liturgical formulas tell us that, at least normally, prayers were not improvised. The *Didache* in fact gives fixed forms for baptism,[19] the Eucharist,[20] and daily prayer,[21] for which a doxology was added to Our Father which found its way back into several codices of Matthew (so fixed was the prayer that liturgical usage could even introduce a non-authentic text into the codices of the New Testament itself: fresh proof that usage was uniformly imposed).

Another important text by reason of its antiquity is the Prayer of the dying St Polycarp. According to Kretschmar,[22] this prayer is an obvious copy of a eucharistic prayer. Now if ever spontaneity is called for, it would seem to be at the moment of death, and not even in this extreme case was the traditional prayer abandoned in favour of improvising a spontaneous one. The strength of this argument is not reduced by saying that the prayer we have owes more to the compiler of the *Deeds of the Martyrs* than to the martyr himself, since the same point is made whether it was the martyr who used a traditional formula or the chronicler who considered it more authentic to put not a spontaneous prayer but one habitual in the community—or at least a version of this—on the lips of his dying protagonist.

A third document—perhaps less well known—reinforces the point: the *Dispute between Origen and Heraclitus* (185-202). This work is an account, made from notes taken at the time, of a discussion between Origen and Bishop Heraclitus.[23] In order to justify his viewpoint, Origen appeals to the way in which the Church expresses itself in prayer. Among the most significant passages is the following: 'In our worship it is necessary that we should respect the "determinations" (συνθῆχαι). If this is not observed, if the 'determinations' are dispensed with, we will end up by placing everything in doubt. It matters little whether we are dealing with a bishop, a presbyter, a deacon or a layman; if anyone does not observe the 'determinations' he is not taking part in the common worship'. This text gives a very interesting clarification of the fact that, by the end of the second century, not only did the Church have fixed forms of worship, but it also understood clearly that these formularies contained the faith of the Church, as opposed to possible prayers made up by members of the community (whatever their rank) which would only express their personal point of view.

(e) Early evidence for 'improvisation'

The texts alluded to in the previous section could be greatly extended if space permitted, but we still need to see if the early centuries can produce texts indicating the opposite: that completely spontaneous prayers were also used. And it is true that there are texts which seem to show this, so let us look at the three most important pieces of evidence for such a usage.

The oldest is a phrase from the *Didache*: 'Allow the prophets to give thanks as much as they wish' (ὅσχ θέλουσιν).[24] This sentence *can* certainly be interpreted in the sense of improvisation. But it can also have other meanings, such as, 'let them give thanks as often as they wish', or 'let them adapt the prayer already given above as they wish' (which last would be well in keeping with the Judaeo-Christian nature of the whole work). Even if it refers to improvisation in the strict sense of the word, it must be said that the *Didache* gives this possibility of improvising as something exceptional— reserved to the prophets—while giving fixed formulations for the usual ceremonies.

The second text comes from the *Apologia of St Justin*: 'He who presides over the brethren makes his prayers and thanksgiving rise up *according to his powers*' (ὅση δύναμισ αὐτῶ).[25] Of this text, like the preceding one, it must be said that it certainly provides a possible reference to improvisation but no absolute proof. The phrase could have other meanings (vibrant intonation, paraphrases, etc.). Justin himself, it should be remembered, paraphrased the baptismal formula of the *Didache* and Matthew. On the other hand, in other parts of his works, Justin gives the content of the eucharistic prayer—which means that it was not up to the president to say whatever he pleased. So, for example, he states that 'thanks are given for the gifts God has granted us',[26] 'praise is offered to the Father of the universe, through the name of the Son and the Holy Spirit',[27] 'the passion that the Son of God suffered for love of us is recalled'.[28] Such statements surely provide the outline of a well-established anaphora? If this is the case the phrase 'according to his powers' is more likely to relate to the tone and possible paraphrases than to a prayer completely improvised by the celebrant.

The third text is a rubric from the *Apostolic Tradition*. After providing many euchological texts including an anaphora, Hippolytus says: 'In no way is it necessary for the bishop to give thanks repeating the same words, as though he were trying to say them from memory, but each should pray according to his capacity. If one is capable of praying at length and saying a solemn prayer let him do so. But if another in his prayers uses only a moderate length prayer he should not be prevented, provided his prayer is orthodox.'[29] It is impossible to comment in detail on this important text here. Let us just say that Hippolytus puts forward a large number of formulations with the intention that they should be used. Most of these are already old texts.[30] So Hippolytus does not 'create'. The formulas handed down by Tradition were in fact spread throughout the Church, which proves that the Church saw its worship as consisting in these forms of prayer, not in other forms that could be freely improvised. The freedom to which Hippolytus alludes fits well with what we have called 'adaptation',[31] less well with what is generally understood by 'creative improvisation'. His rubric also reflects an atmosphere similar to that of the Jewish 'targums', and indeed the whole of his work, including the rubrics, is strongly marked by Judaic echoes.

(f) Conclusion

Very lengthy conclusions could be drawn from this study, but space allows only a few lines. To sum up briefly: the early centuries did not have organisations which laid down every detail, but this does not mean that everything was left to individual presidents of the assembly; as with Israel, whose liturgy was the main source for Christian worship, the outlines were firmly laid down; the ancient ideal of 'creativity' differed considerably from our ideas of it—and this is perhaps the key for understanding the meaning and import of expressions that seem to favour 'improvisation' in the early centuries: the ideal of the early Christians was to say *always the same thing* with *the most solemn expression possible*: 'Thanks as much as they wish' (*Didache*); 'according to his powers' (Justin); *long* and *solemn* prayer (Hippolytus). The ideal of those who now favour improvisation, on the other hand, would seem to be 'to say new things', not to repeat; to 'create' so as to avoid routine and always to be interesting by virtue of the novelty of the prayers. I think these are two very different worlds.

Translated by Paul Burns

Notes

1. So, for example, Botte and Vögel *Introduction aux sources de l'histoire du culte chrétien au Moyen Age* (Spoleto 1966) p. 20; at first sight they seem to confirm this view, but in fact the way they develop the subject shows that they are very far from referring to improvisation in the modern sense of the term.
2. On this, see *Sacr. Conc.* n. 21.
3. See M.-L. Rouquette *La Créativité* (Coll. *Que sais-je?*, no. 1528, Paris 1976) p. 120.
4. n. 50.
5. n. 4.
6. nn. 37-40.
7. *Ibid.*
8. See, e.g., the allocutions of Paul VI to the *Concilium* of 13 October 1966 and 10 April 1970; Directory for Masses for Children, no. 3; *Instructio de interpretatione textuum liturgicorum* of 25 January 1969, etc.
9. See folio 11.
10. See, e.g., the frequent rubric, '*his vel similibus verbis*'.
11. Alternate edition, p. 879.
12. It is generally agreed by exegetes today that the purpose of many of the New Testament writings was to be read in the liturgical assemblies; see, e.g., 1 Thess. 4:27; Col. 4:16.
13. As, e.g., the accounts of the Last Supper and, possibly, some of the hymns included in the letters of the Apostles and the Apocalypse.
14. This is true of the medieval hymnody for the office, for example, which included more than 30,000 hymns.

15. See *Sacr. Conc.* n. 21.
16. See the texts from the *Didache*, Justin and Hippolytus below.
17. See Hruby *Eucharisties d'Orient et d'Occident* (Paris 1970) p. 42.
18. *Idem.*, p. 43.
19. VII, 1.
20. IX-X (I am leaving out here the question of whether this refers to a Christian or a Jewish Eucharist).
21. VIII, 2-3.
22. See the summary of his intervention on the twenty-fifth anniversary of the Institut Supérieur of Paris, published in *Questions liturgiques*, 1982, I, p. 11.
23. See M. Quasten *Patrology* (Utrecht-Brussels), Vol. I.
24. X, 7.
25. *Apologia* I, 67, 4.
26. *Ibid.* I, 65, 3.
27. *Ibid.*
28. *Dialogue with Tryphon*, 117, 4.
29. Botte *La Tradition apostolique* (Münster 1963) p. 29, no. 9.
30. Kretschmar, the article cited in note 22, p. 9.
31. See folios 8-10.

Charles Pietri

Liturgy, Culture and Society: The Example of Rome at the End of the Ancient World (Fourth-Fifth Centuries)

FOR THE historian, liturgy is, among other things, a social and cultural phenomenon. Of course, an observer, whatever his private attitude, cannot ignore all the implied references to the sacred contained in collective prayer, but at the same time he notes how Christians make use of contemporary environment for the structure, language and gestures of divine service. This awareness protects him from the naïve pretensions of an apologetic which, since Chateaubriand, has been proclaiming the original genius of a religion and its rights, but he also needs prudence to avoid the reductionist comparativism of a whole school of history of religion at the end of the last century, which plunged the Christian liturgy into a confused syncretism, stressing all that its rites, festivals and sacrifices had borrowed from mystery religions and paganism. In the analysis of the interchange of influences between pagan antiquity, the Jewish tradition and Christianity, F. J. Dölger has opened up a magisterial path for research: *Antike und Christentum* is the title of six collections published by this learned professor from Bonn and of an encyclopedia which continues his work.[1]

This work, by dint of precise investigations, has begun to construct a synthesis the results of which become particularly appreciable as the investigation reaches the period of the Christian empire, the fourth and fifth centuries, a time when conversion, at least in the towns, was becoming a mass phenomenon. A variety of influences was now acting on the cultural and social development both of the Christian laity and of its clergy. In return for the ending of the persecutions, political protection and even limited economic assistance, the clergy had to accept the irksome interference of a Christian emperor who declared himself from time to time 'bishop of bishops'. At the same time conversions increasingly reached the social élite and, finally, in the fifth century, the majority of the aristocracy, bringing into the Church a rich heritage of culture, forms of behaviour and ideological attitudes. Furthermore, this Church, having emerged from the anguish of the persecution, readily attributed a providential role to the prince and the empire, together with its political and social system.

Of course it would be a mistake (though one often made today) to do no more than anathemise this 'Constantinian' Church.[2] It is a Church which may seem compromised and established in the world, but it also gave rise to the powerful monastic movement which continued, in the eyes of the world, the witness begun by the martyrs. It organised the first system of collective poor relief, so marking the recognition of the poor, who had for so long been excluded from history. It produced Palatine prelates, but also champions of religious freedom, Athanasius and Hilary, John Chrysostom and Pope Innocent, and, out of the beneficial explosion of theological controversies, the fathers of a new Christian thought, from the Cappadocians to Augustine of Hippo.

In the texture of such a manifestly complex historical phenomenon, it is difficult to distinguish, in the interaction of *Antike* and *Christentum*, between deliberate borrowings, the use of a common language of trivialised gestures, concepts and symbols, and examples of the infiltration of alien practices which indicate an undue influence on the part of the social and cultural environment. This ambiguity is clearly illustrated in the production of Christian artists. When they reproduce the image of the sleeping Endymion to illustrate the sleep of Jonah, they are looking for a convenient model without trying to establish a connection between the prophet and the son of Zeus. But the mosaic artist and the sculptor who represent the Lord also use insignia, gestures or structures codified by iconography to denote the imperial power, and the borrowing seems less innocent in view of all that the parallel can contribute to the image of the prince, the reflection of the celestial emperor. But the artist is both freer in his choice and more dependent on his lay clients, except in the decoration of churches. In the direction of the liturgy the clergy exercised a direct control and firmly maintained the weight of a tradition. The Roman Church provides a uniquely valuable example of this particular development because it is easier in Rome than elsewhere to follow the social history of a conversion and to trace its success through the fourth and fifth centuries. It is true that we often lack the most important texts of the Roman liturgy. Hippolytus' *Apostolic Tradition* dates from a century before the Constantinian settlement,[3] and, while the sacramentaries,[4] the Leonine, the Gelasian and particularly the Gregorian, almost certainly contain formulas which may go back to the fifth century, the identification of the older prayers in these late compilations is often a delicate business. Fortunately literature (especially the letters of the popes) and archaeology provide enough evidence to follow the process of cultural and social adaptation in the development of liturgy. They also make it possible to identify, in the aims of pastoral work, the image the local church had of itself in the midst of this new world.

1. A CONQUEST OF URBAN SPACE

The study of this adaptation must begin with the outward signs, which are the most obvious. From the beginning of the fourth century, the liturgy had received a new setting in which to mount its rites and assemble its people in prayer. Then, thanks to this material base created by imperial generosity and the donations of a converted aristocracy, the pastors developed, more and more clearly, the idea of a genuine conquest of urban space which would establish specialised buildings for collective prayer throughout the city and its periphery.

In the case of Rome we must recognise at least one benefit (no doubt the most substantial) of the new policy inaugurated after 312 by Constantine. With the Lateran basilica the prince gave Rome, or rather its bishop, the first great hall for Christian liturgy. The identity of the founder, who made the gift in the first decade of his reign, and certainly before 324, is confirmed by a papal chronicle of the sixth century, the *Liber Pontificalis*, which contains a foundation charter listing the lands, the various liturgical vessels and the lights given by the emperor to this *basilica constantiniana*. The new building was erected, not on the site of a palace, as was sometimes thought, but in the area of an élite cavalry barracks, formerly occupied by an aristocratic residence, that of the *Laterani*, whose memory was still preserved by the name of the site in the fourth century. The basilica (now St John Lateran), offered the Christians of Rome a grand setting, a grand building,[5] as imposing as the civil basilica in Trajan's forum, as the Temple of Venus and Rome. The building of this church transformed the setting of the liturgy. It gave it a permanent establishment, capable of containing for the first time in Rome the people gathered round their bishop in a single collective act of prayer.

Even more than this direct physical effect of bringing people together, the monumentalisation of the liturgical setting changed the style of worship. We should not try to establish too close a connection between architecture and ritual. It is not possible to distinguish in the building of the episcopal basilica the influence of clergy with a clear programme and that of the architects creating a synthesis out of diverse elements in which technical constraints were as important as the desire to use a grandiose imperial language for this monument. Nevertheless, such a building did mark out a new space for the liturgy. It made possible processions; it gave emphasis to particular areas, the royal way with its special lighting and the inner naves, while the outermost naves were darker. In the transept, near the altar, there was space for seven offertory tables, while the apse became the site of the bishop's chair, placed facing the people at the East end.[6] The pastor also now had a building organised for baptism less than a hundred yards from the cathedral. The round baptistry, which received annexes, especially in the fifth century, was huge enough (its diameter only a little less than that of the Pantheon) to allow the sacrament of the integration of new Christians to become a social event in the presence of the whole believing people.

In two centuries (particularly in the fourth and at the beginning of the fifth) new buildings sprang up all over the urban area; for his liturgy the bishop now had a basilica on the Esquiline (Sta Maria Maggiore). Over the whole territory of Rome churches were housing local liturgical gatherings; each of them had an endowment guaranteeing the maintenance of the building and its clergy and possessed liturgical equipment including lights and the sacred vessels. A foundation charter, the *titulus* or 'title', established, in law and fact, the permanence of the church. These titles were created at random, as the donations came, in the names of bishops (the title of Mark, Julius, Liberius, etc.), in those of lay people, aristocrats (Lucina, Sabina, Crescens, Vestina, etc.). In other cases the collections may have tapped the pennies of the poor for the work.[7] Finally this anarchic process created a complete network of liturgical buildings: in the fifth century few Christian dwellings were more than 500 yards from a building dedicated to the synaxis and the sacraments. It was the period when authority forbade pagan sacrifices and closed the temples which housed the ancient idols. In the City there was now only a single presence, public and official, for the celebration of sacred rites, that of the churches which had conquered the urban space.

Churches also appeared on the outskirts, near the tombs of the martyrs. Imperial generosity (especially that of Constantine) made possible the construction of a sort of monumental housing for the tomb of Peter at the Vatican, and for Paul's on the Ostian Way. Beside Laurence's grave on the Tiburtine Way and Agnes' on the Via Nomentana, huge basilicas sheltered the devotions and the graves of the faithful. In the cemeteries the bishops (especially Damasus, 366-384) created space for pilgrimage and for collective prayer near the graves. Rome was surrounded by a garland of buildings available to this movement of spirituality which celebrated the memory of the martyrs. From the centre to the outskirts these two networks complemented each other: from the middle of the fourth century the bishops used for their large liturgical gatherings the basilicas of the apostles, in particular that of Peter at the Vatican, where the pope, from the time of Liberius (352-365), celebrated Christmas. In all these ways this monumental establishment gave a new style to Christian assemblies: they now brought together a more numerous community in permanent centres constructed for prayer.

2. CHRISTIAN TIME

At the same time pastoral strategy quite deliberately multiplied these assemblies. From Constantine onwards the law aided this conquest of time by prohibiting civil activities and profane celebrations on the 'Sun's day', which was finally named 'the Lord's day' (*dies dominica*).[8] But the bishop did not use his new cathedral merely to assemble his people in the Sunday *synaxis*; he also made it a key centre in the organisation of a liturgical year. For three weeks in the fourth century, the Church fasted with the catechumens; in the fifth century the length of this period of community instruction and ascesis was increased to forty days.[9] The organisation of Holy Week—a legal holiday from 389—is better known. There was a gathering on the Wednesday at which—according to the late evidence of an *ordo Romanus*—the *orationes solemnes* were recited. The bishop gathered the faithful on Thursday to reconcile the penitents: as early as the fourth century the group of penitents obliged to submit themselves to public humiliation had begun to dissolve into discrete individuals. In the fourth century from the Friday to Easter Day the cathedral and its baptistry remained the centre for prayer and the sacrament of baptism: this practice further reinforced the 'socialisation' of the 'ritual of integration'. The candidate—perhaps on Holy Saturday—submitted to a public profession of faith because the Church gave this commitment a solemn character by inviting the catechumen to recite the creed before the assembled faithful. Occasions for these assemblies multiplied, and once the bishop had large basilicas at his disposal he was able to move, with his people, from the east of his city to the west and so lay the foundations of a stational liturgy. As early as the middle of the fourth century St Peter's was the scene of the celebration of the Nativity and, half a century later, that of Epiphany; around the same period, probably in Leo's time, the celebrations of the forty and fifty days after Easter took shape, once again held in the west, in the Vatican building.[10]

The supporting role of the titular churches established in the different districts of Rome became more and more important as conversions increased the numbers of the community of believers and the practice of frequent communion became established. One rite in particular emphasises the ties between the local liturgy and the celebration presided over by the bishop. As Bishop Innocent (402-417) explains (*ep.* 25, 5, 8), the priests received for their celebration the papal *fermentum*, a particle of bread consecrated by the pope, and, in a gesture of unity, placed it in the chalice as a sort of leaven for their sacrifice. The titular churches did not have a territory like the later urban parishes, but they did become the usual place of Christian assembly and reinforced the pastoral strategy based on the idea of Christian time. The cycle of the episcopal liturgy was developed by the addition of their feasts in honour of the saint who protected them or whose relics they housed—the chains, for example, in the case of St Peter ad Vincula. Pope Leo invited the faithful to bring their offerings for the communal collection during the times of fasting (June and September) to the titular church. And an even more significant detail should be noted. The author of a theological treatise (the *Praedestinatus*), who must have been a contemporary of Pope Sixtus (432-440), mentions for the first time the nuptial mass. The network of the *tituli* had made it possible to move from the family home to the church a ceremony which had originally been private but now became a public commitment, contracted in the presence of the believing community.[11]

This pastoral structure was completed by the organisation of ferials, celebrations of

D

the memory of the saints in the great basilicas of the martyrs (like St Peter's), in the titular churches in the fifth century and above all on the tombs of the martyrs on the outskirts of the City. At the beginning of the fourth century the Christian community of Rome had an official calendar listing thirty martyrs (the *Depositio Martyrum*) and setting aside each year for the commemoration of the saints twenty days, for the most part grouped by the accidents of the persecution between July and September. From the middle of the fourth century Damasus and his successors chose from the many popular devotions those which allowed the liturgical year to be extended, to January, June, October, outside the seasons of Easter and Christmas. In this way the Church filled up the empty spaces in the liturgical cycle. The Christian celebration sometimes coincided with one of the pagan feasts. Perhaps the coincidence was accidental. The bishops, contrary to the interpretation beloved by students of folklore, did not attempt to Christianise pagan feasts. In fact Christian pastoral strategy popularised the anniversary of a saint, revived his or her memory with an official celebration, in order to divert the faithful on that day from the circus and its attractions. The feast of Priscilla, Abdon and Sennen were placed in July after that of Peter and Paul (29 June): it would be a happy coincidence if the Christian gathering distracted the faithful from the *ludi apollinares*, the games celebrated in honour of Apollo (5-14 July).

3. LANGUAGES AND GESTURES

This pastoral strategy based on space and time did not necessarily change the structure of the synaxis or the organisation of the baptismal rite. But it created a new atmosphere for collective prayer; it imposed a style, adaptations which apparently affected the most superficial manifestations of the liturgy, its language and its gestures. During the first centuries the celebrant and the faithful spoke Greek. Greek was doubtless the language of the first missionaries and certainly that of the majority of the faithful; it was the language used by Clement of Rome and, towards the middle of the second century, by Hermas, the author of a short apocalypse, though here Latinisms begin to appear. At the beginning of the following century Hippolytus was still using Greek to produce his treatises and his little manual of discipline and liturgy, the *Apostolic Tradition*. Around 250, however, Novatian, with an air of theological authority, quite naturally used Latin to write a treatise *On the Trinity*. From the third to the fourth centuries funerary inscriptions reflect this Latinisation of Roman Christianity, with the gradual decrease of Greek inscriptions, with the use of Greek characters to transcribe Latin texts and finally, in the last cemeteries to be developed, with a considerable increase of Latin inscriptions. In the West, in Africa from the end of the second century, and also in Rome, Christians were speaking and writing a Latin which possessed a specialised vocabulary, particular turns of phrase, a creativity of its own, which has been identified by the studies of T. Schrijnen and the monumental work of C. Mohrmann.[12] This Christian Latin borrowed from Greek and even, via Greek, from Hebrew: *pascha, epiphania, episcopus, diaconus*. It gave words specialised meanings by diverting them from their current usage; *caritas* is one example. Under the influence of biblical Greek *praedicare* was used intransitively to refer to preaching and *refrigerare* came to denote happiness in the next world. Some semiological changes took longer to become established: *paganus* to denote the pagan and not just the inhabitant of the *pagus*, *sermo* for the sermon, *basilica* for the vast space of the great churches. The new meanings may overlap: *statio*, the word for a sentry's post, denotes both the penitential rite and the assembly in a church, and *confessio*, which, in Tertullian, means confession of sins, also recalls the resistance of the confessor of the faith and, finally, praise, under the influence of the Latin psalter (Ps. 117). Christian creativity is also reflected in numerous neologisms (*salvator, cooperator*), in a language totally uninterested in elegance of strict rules. This Latin did not shrink from phrases borrowed from oral style or modelled on Greek: adjectives of belonging (*apostolica traditio*), the adnominal genitive (*dies iudicii*, the day on which the judgment will take place). Pastoral needs made the most urgent task the translation of the Bible into Latin; very soon the theologians and the polemicists used this Latin, with very little further refinement, to fight heresy or fortify faith and morals.

When the Roman liturgy began to use Christian Latin, this dynamic and creative language had been in the making for almost two centuries. A. Baumstark expressed his amazement at this in a paper published shortly before the war; he believed that the first translations of the canon went back to the period of Pope Cornelius (251-253).[13] But these hypotheses conflict with the evidence of a philosopher, established and baptised in Rome, Marius Victorinus, who, around 360, quotes in Greek a few words from a prayer from the anaphora (*oratio oblationis*). To defend against the elders the use of the word ὁμοούσιος, he chose a text evidently known to all, explaining that the Roman liturgy used expressions very close to the term adopted by the council of Nicea: Σῶσον περιουσιον λαον ζηλοτεν καλῶν, 'Save the people gathered round the substance, which means,' explained Victorinus, 'round life, as it says in the prayer of offering' (*Contre Arius*, ed. Hadot, p. 417). A few years later a contemporary of Pope Damasus (366-384), Ambrosiaster, the obscure author of *Quaestiones Veteris et Novi Testamenti*, quoted a prayer from the canon, in Latin this time. He was protesting against the title *summus sacerdos* given to Melchisedek, 'sicut nostri in oblatione praesumunt', 'as our people (the faithful of Rome),' he explains, 'mistakenly do in the anaphora' (*Quaest.* 109, 20; Vogel p. 246). These two sources mark a decisive stage in Rome, one which had taken place after 360, in the second half of the century. The second source, however, in his commentary on 1 Corinthians (1:14), suggests that the change of liturgical language met solid resistance. He contrasts, following Paul, the prophet who speaks for the edification of the people with the speaker in tongues. If you come together to build up the Church, he says, you must use words which all the hearers understand; some imitate the Jews, who use Hebrew in preference to Aramaic (*syra lingua*): 'They would address the people at prayer in a language they did not know rather than in their own.' The insistence of this exegesis on interpreting speaking in tongues as the use of a liturgical language unfamliar to the people quite probably reflects the fierceness of a recent debate. In other words, the Roman Church had been slow to follow the linguistic development of a people which had long contained a Latin-speaking majority. The adaptation became essential at the moment when the clergy were more and more able to exemplify the unity of the Christian people in the city churches, by their efficient organisation of the calendar of community assemblies. From that moment pastoral needs, as conversions swelled to a flood, made it necessary to abandon Greek, which to some extent had the position of a sacred language: *ad aedificandam ecclesiam*, to build up the unity of the local church, as Ambrosiaster explains.

The adoption of Latin amounted to a concession to popular education, but the clergy had no intention of abandoning the dignity and solemnity of sacred expression in prayer. Henceforth the people might understand, but to address God, as Hilary of Poitiers (*Tractat. in Ps.* XIII, 1) recommended in Gaul, the celebrant could not use the humble language of every day. This insistence, which had doubtless been used to support Greek before the adoption of Latin, made itself strongly felt when the Roman community was reinforced by the converted aristocracy and, with it, by a culture, habits of speech, a whole system of reference to the ancient Roman tradition. This is the period in which, under this influence, the panegyric of the Christian City began to use, to celebrate the primacy of an apostolic see, language which had formerly lauded the ancient capital, *Roma sacra*, that Rome made sacred henceforward by real holiness. It is impossible to say, for want of evidence dated with certainty, if the editors of the Latin prayers fixed the features and style of this specialised liturgical Latin all at once. Very probably the hierarchy quickly drew up a common text for the anaphora which was then used in all the City's assemblies,[14] and gradually regulated, before finally eliminating, the freedom to improvise which the celebrant long retained in the prefaces and the prayers preceding and following the canon. In the sacramentaries (beginning with the Leonine), collectors complete the model of the prayer proper to each celebration. To measure this development of Latin which took place between the fourth and sixth centuries it is enough to compare the text of the canon preserved in the Gelasian sacramentary with the prayer reported in Ambrose's *De Sacramentis*. Ambrose's text, substantially identical with the Roman canon, preserves in its doublets the freedom of oral style which contrasts with the hieratic rigour of the former.[15] The Roman editors purged the popular language of the Latin Christians; while they might keep the indispensable terms (*paschalia, ecclesia*), they aimed at the noble style of the ancient Roman prayers (*celebrare, dicare, immolare*), and used *preces* and *pontifex* rather than *oratio* and *episcopus* to refer to prayer and the bishop. They borrowed the language of the imperial chancery to talk to God, *maiestas*, or the celebration, *officium*, and did not shrink from the legal precision of official terminology: *commendare, intercedere, munus*. In playing on alliteration and the balancing of symmetrical elements, they borrowed from literary prose: *rogamus ac petimus, omnis honor et gloria, praeceptis salutaribus moniti et divina institutione formati*. And in the prayers of the sacramentaries they even intimated the structure of ancient pagan prayers which combine laudatory invocation with the precise demand of the petition. In these more recent texts the prose has a rhythm based on a *cursus* which plays with metre and stress to give the prayers, like the sermons of Popes Celestine and Leo, like the decretals, the stately cadence of imperial texts.

To accompany this rhetorical prayer uttered in a triumphal setting, court ritual inspired a whole symbolism of gesture,[16] the celebrant's prostration before the divine majesty at the beginning of the assembly (*Ord. Rom.* 1, 8), the assessor calling for silence before the readings of Scripture as the *silentiarii* did in the palace of the Caesars (Gelasian I, 31). At court etiquette required that the subject received the written order given by the prince with his hands covered: the subdeacon received the Gospel *super planetam*, his hands covered by the chasuble (*Ord. Rom.* 1, 11). Those who approached the altar had to wear more magnificent clothes than the people, the *vestes sacratae* referred to in the papal chronicle. Palatine pomp imposed analogous rules, but the dress of the clergy does not yet seem to have become specialised, except for the deacon's dalmatic, attested with certainty, and the pallium, the broad band of white wool round the shoulders, from the end of the fifth century. Still other rites borrowed from princely ceremonial: in the cathedral itself the *ciborium* protected the altar like the canopy over the imperial throne, and the incense which accompanied the entry (*adventus*) of the ruler and his triumphal procession also burned for the celestial emperor. Jerome refers to the practice of lighting candles during the reading of Scripture as was done for the presentation of imperial documents (*Contra Vigilantium* 7).

The faithful, too, punctuated the communal prayer with their codified acclamations, and the Amen used to burst like thunder, Jerome says, in the Roman basilicas. In this the Christians were following the Jews, the pagan rituals, but also official discipline. Acclamations[17] punctuated meetings of councils as they did sessions of the senate; in church an intervention like *Dignum et iustum est* (introduced at an early date) may belong to the ritual for the proclamation of a prince, like the acclamation which celebrated the long reign promised to Caesar. From the fifth century, the *Liber pontificalis* suggests, the entry was organised as a majestic procession accompanied by the deacons singing psalms. In the liturgy of the Lateran, however, where the interior was designed to allow the people to move, the offertory procession involved the laity as well as the clergy; everyone brought their offerings to one of the seven tables placed in the transept. The conversion of the aristocracy and the importance of Christian benefactions which supported the charitable and organisational work of the church undoubtedly explain the importance given to the offertory ceremony. A prayer said—*inter mysteria*—over the offerings solemnly mentioning the donors (or the most generous ones) reminded the faithful of their obligations. For the Church's pastoral strategy associating the people as a whole with the work of charity was just as important as demonstrating unity in this procession towards the bishop. This ritual too, however, owed something to the fixed gestures of the homage rendered to the prince. The prince received from his subjects gold for his crown; the believer brought to the alter a circlet of bread.

This whole process concerned only indirectly the content of the prayer, with the exception of the prayer responding to the offertory procession; this formed part of a canon the organisation of which was completely fixed in the sixth century. Nevertheless the process does reflect the debt of liturgical creativity in the Roman Church to contemporary culture and society. These changes reflect the ambitions of a victorious pastoral strategy which had become surer of its resources and more confident of success in managing a mass Church. At the same time it gave the celebration of the celestial emperor many of the features, gestures and words associated with the ruling prince of the Christian empire. In these complementary movements can be discerned the faint outline of the future 'Christendom'.

Translated by Francis McDonagh

Notes

1. Six volumes, 1929-1950; see T. Klauser, Franz-Joseph Dölger (1879-1940) *Jahrbuch für Antike und Christentum*, Ergänzungsheft (supplementary vol.), Münster 1980.
2. C. Pietri 'Mythe et réalité de l'Eglise constantienne' *Les Quatre Fleuves* 3 (1974) 22-39.
3. Ed. B. Botte *Liturg. Quellen* 39 (Münster 1963).
4. L. C. Mohlberg *Liber sacramentorum Rom. Ecclesiae ordinis anni circuli (sacramentarium gelasianum)* (Rome 1960); similarly for the 'Leonine': *Sacramentum Veronense* (Rome 1966).
5. C. Pietri *Roma Christiana. Recherches sur l'Eglise de Rome, son organisation, sa politique, son idéologie de Miltiade à Sixte III (311-440)* (Rome 1976) 2 vols.
6. *Liber pontificalis* ed. L. Duchesne (Paris 1955) pp. 172ff.
7. *Roma Christiana* I, pp. 14ff; pp. 461-573.
8. W. Rordorf *Sabbat et dimanche dans l'Eglise ancienne*, French trans. (Neufchatel 1972).
9. See the studies by A. Chavasse mentioned in C. Vogel *Introduction aux sources de l'histoire du culte chrétien au Moyen Age*, Centro italiano de Studi sull'alto medioevo (Spoleto 1966) pp. 269-274.
10. *Roma Christiana* I, pp. 589ff; pp. 586ff; p. 115, etc.
11. On the pastoral strategy of the *tituli*, *ibid.* 628.
12. See the essays collected in C. Mohrmann *Etudes sur le latin des Chrétiens, Storia e Letteratura* (Rome 1958) I; (1961) II; (1965) III; (1971) IV.
13. On the whole debate, T. Klauser 'Der Übergang der römischen Kirche von der griechischen zur lateinischen Liturgiesprache' *Gesammelte Arbeiten* ed. E. Dassmann (Münster 1970) pp. 184-194.
14. For the concern for the unity of the celebration, see the rite of the *fermentum*.

46   LITURGY, CULTURE AND SOCIETY

15. B. Botte *L'Ordinaire de la messe* (Louvain 1953) p. 111; *ibid.* C. Mohrmann, pp. 40ff; see also *Latin Chrétien* II, pp. 102ff; M. P. Ellebracht *Remarks on the vocabulary of the ancient Orations in the Missale Romanum* (Nijmegen 1963).

16. Known mainly from the *Ordines Romani* published by M. Andrieu, Louvain, 5 vols., 1931-1956. It is reasonable to suppose that in this area these later texts have preserved an ancient ritual. On court ritual, see A. Alföldi *Die monarchische Repräsentation im röm Kaiserreich* (Darmstadt 1970).

17. T. Klauser 'Akklamation' *Reallexikon für Antike und Christentum* I, 216f.

James White

Creativity: The Free Church Tradition

TENS OF millions of Americans assemble each Sunday for worship according to one variety or another of the most popular worship tradition in the United States, the Free Church. Despite its popular appeal, the Free Church worship tradition remains the least studied by liturgical scholars and is frequently ignored altogether. Yet no concern with liturgical creativity can overlook the tradition which provides the maximum possibility for originality and inventiveness.

1. THE TRADITION AND ITS AMERICAN DEVELOPMENT

I shall first define what I mean by the 'Free Church worship tradition' especially in the context of American Christianity where it is dominant. There its influence has reached far beyond its historical borders and decisively shaped worship within Methodist, Reformed, and Pentecostal traditions as well. The Free Church worship tradition encompasses groups as varied as Southern Baptists, Disciples of Christ, or Seventh Day Adventists. Yet common factors unite these groups in worship despite disparity in theology, ethics, and institutions.

Almost all Protestant worship stands within one of seven distinct liturgical traditions. These reflect the left, central, and right wings of the Reformation developing over five centuries.

Century	Left Wing	Centre	Right Wing
16th	A[1] *Free Church:* Continental Anabaptist	B. Reformed	C. Lutheran D. Anglican
17th	E. Quaker A[2] *Free Church:* English Puritan		
18th		F. Methodist	
19th	A[3] *Free Church:* American Frontier		
20th	G. Pentecostal		

47

As can be seen, the Free Church tradition is manifest in three historically-diverse circumstances: one shaped by attempts to complete the Reformation in the sixteenth century, a second to purify a national church in the seventeenth, and another to Christianise a continent in the nineteenth. To a certain extent, each group was successful in accomplishing these goals although historical differences demanded different stresses. I shall limit myself to the third of these, the American frontier manifestation.

We still understand relatively little about the process of the Americanisation of Protestant worship. The nineteenth century marked a major watershed between the Reformation and present-day Protestant worship. Even the term 'Free Church' in its original Puritan usage meant free to follow God's Word; but it came to have an entirely different meaning, namely freedom to do as one pleased in shaping worship. The major growth of the Free Church tradition in America occurred among people who had fled organised and settled regions of the country for the freedom of the frontier. Service books were unknown and unmissed; the ordering of worship often depended upon a local minister who might be a farmer the rest of the week or an itinerant preacher.

The most representative person in nineteenth-century American Protestantism was Charles G. Finney (1792-1875). He disdained traditional methods of worship in favour of 'new measures' that reflected the religious needs and emotions of those who flocked to camp meetings on the frontier or revivals in settled regions. In the process of using such measures, the Free Church tradition became Americanised. It also came to have a heavy impact on Methodist and Reformed traditions. Already in 1792, Methodists had abandoned a service book except for 'sacramental services'; and Presbyterians operated with no more restraint.

Certain general features remain characteristic of Free Church worship in America. First, the Eucharist is an occasional service rather than the usual service except among Disciples of Christ and the Churches of Christ. Even in these churches, the use of service books other than hymnals is rare and the order of worship varies from congregation to congregation. Second, most of these churches are antipaedobaptist although the United Church of Christ or the United Church of Canada would be exceptions. The attitude towards sacraments (if that term is even used instead of 'ordinances') derives largely from the desacralising influence of the Enlightenment wed to a biblicism. Sacraments are viewed as pious memory exercises, commanded by Scripture, rather than as means of grace.

Third, most churches in the Free Church tradition are congregationalist in polity, acknowledging little central authority in church government and still less in worship. Each congregation is free to order its worship as it feels best. They thus provide a fascinating variety to study but it is exasperatingly difficult to generalise about anything liturgical since each congregation represents only itself. There is much that is common but none of it obligatory such as is the use of service books among Lutherans or Episcopalians. The liturgical life of this tradition remains little explored primarily because of the difficulty of studying so many thousands of local expressions of Free Church worship.

2. STRUCTURE AND CREATIVITY: FIVE MOMENTS

Nevertheless, I shall make some generalisations about the possibilities for creativity in this tradition and then proceed to evaluate the actual results. The most important opportunity for creativity in Free Church worship comes in the *ordering of worship*. Either in the total absence of any denominational ordo or despite the presence of such, worship in the Free Church tradition allows each congregation to determine its own order of worship. There will be variety in the order of worship not only from congregation to congregation but from Sunday to Sunday. No particular order is considered normative or permanent.

Although the original goal of English Puritanism's struggle was for the freedom to order worship according to God's word, i.e., authenticity, the chief concern today seems to be relevance. Each congregation and each occasion is different. Never do exactly the same people gather again amidst the same world situation. Even the third Sunday of Easter and the fourth are different occasions in the world community and in the local church. Therefore one ought to be able to order worship specifically for the here and now of particular people on a specific occasion. The order of worship ought to be as up-to-date as the morning newspaper and to reflect the local community equally well.

If the ordering of worship is recognised as providing opportunity for making the service relevant to a specific people and time, it is not as widely recognised that the order is also an important theological statement. This the Puritans saw clearly. What one does and says and the sequence in which this happens does much to shape the faith and spirituality of the congregation. (A photograph of the Statue of Liberty says one thing next to one of the Golden Gate, something else next to one of Red Square.) A service that begins with the Apostles' Creed says something quite different about the source of faith than one in which the creed follows the reading and preaching of God's Word. Unfortunately, the importance of the order of worship as theological statement is often overlooked. Yet the order is the theological document (usually in mimeographed or printed form) most frequently laid before the worshippers. The order is far more important in the congregation's formation than it might seem from its use as a throw-away guide to that day's service of worship. Greater awareness of this function of the order of worship might lead to greater care in its construction.

Frequently pastors or worship committees deliberately vary the order of worship from week to week. Two incentives to creativity seem to operate. Many are convinced that people are more attentive when variety is present, a factor hard to deny. Increasingly such variety is more and more guided by the liturgical year. The widespread move to use of the ecumenical lectionary (in various versions of the Roman Catholic Sunday lectionary) has led to fuller observance of Christological festivals. These have provided a row of pegs on which to hang creative ideas. Thus the order may include a much heavier penitential emphasis during Lent than during Easter or the location of a prayer of confession may vary or disappear according to the season.

The order may be varied to enhance the meaning of the sermon on the specific occasion. Thus, according to the lections and sermons, the response to the Word can range from creed to hymn, prayer of confession, or act of offering.

Despite the fear of a stereotyped form of service, which motivates many pastors to attempt some variety in the order of worship from week to week, basic patterns endure. Given such possibilities, there is less variety than one might expect. For example, among Methodists in the South, an order of worship dating from 1905 seems still to be in widespread use and is only slightly varied locally. But the ideal is there: a magnificent opportunity to work creatively to order worship so as to gain the maximum degree of relevance for each service.

In every tradition, the *sermon* is probably the most obvious occasion for creativity. Only the Hutterites seem to prefer sermons drawn from the past rather than those prepared for the present. In Free Church worship, the sermon tends to be the dominant element even when the Eucharist is celebrated. Thus the sermon is crucial in shaping the order of worship and in determining all of its components. This may be more prevalent when a lectionary is not used. When a thematic or topical approach to preaching prevails, there is a tendency to chose all the propers to relate to the subject at hand:

forgiveness, tithing, prayer, or whatever. Though often subject to overloading, a certain amount of coherence results in each service and the distinctive character of each occasion is clearly manifest.

A third opportunity for creativity in the Free Church tradition occurs in the so-called *'pastoral prayer'*. Various English Puritans objected to the fixed collects of the *Book of Common Prayer* as not dynamic enough to cover the ever-changing spectrum of human existence and as 'stinted' prayers because of their brevity. Their alternative, finally defined in the *Westminster Directory* of 1644, was an all-purpose prayer that tried to be comprehensive in summing up the concerns of the congregation. In the twentieth century, it has become known as the 'pastoral prayer'. Essentially it is a long prayer that changes from week to week in which the pastor sums up the concerns of his or her congregation. It is based on intimate pastoral knowledge of the fears and anxieties, the joys and hopes of a specific people. Thus it can do what the prayers of the faithful do in Roman Catholic worship but it also can do much more. Frequently it combines confession and oblation, petition and intercession. It has clear parallels to the eucharistic prayer of Justin Martyr's time in which the pastor prays to the best of his ability for the people and the congregation assents to such prayer with its 'Amen'.

There is much variety in the preparation of the pastoral prayer. Some pastors rely on spontaneity as if any preparation would be a cramping of the Holy Spirit. They seem oblivious to John Wesley's comment about the irony of carefully preparing sermons for us worms and praying to Almighty God with no preparation. Others spend considerable time in preparation for such prayer, recalling their pastoral visits of the previous week, reflecting the *Westminster Directory*'s suggestion of rehearsing 'the Cheife and most usefull heads of the Sermon', and surveying current events in the local community. A few pastors spend as much time in preparation of the pastoral prayer as on their sermon. They are the exception but congregations know who they are and frequently attend to hear such prayer. At the other extreme are pastoral prayers that are simply hackneyed repetitions of the same pious clichés week after week. Even worse, some yield to the temptation to include parish announcements within such prayer, a practice often betrayed by slippage into third person language rather than 'you, God'.

The supreme advantage of a good pastoral prayer is the opportunity to be creative in expressing the situation in time and space of a particular people. It can give voice to their unexpressed feelings with both authenticity and relevancy. By giving such expression, it helps a community affirm its very existence before God. And one should not be reluctant to acknowledge the enormous catechetical value such prayer has in instructing people how to pray in personal devotions. Teaching people how to pray is the very essence of pastoral care and the pastoral prayer can be a magnificent exemplar. A similar challenge to creativity occurs in the preparation of other types of prayers: confession, opening prayer, invocations, and oblation.

Choice of the various propers—hymns, psalms, and lections—provides a fourth chance for creativity. Many pastors see this selection process as a prime opportunity to give continuity to a service. A few advocate Scripture read in *lectio continua* fashion; most chose their own portions or follow a lectionary. Hymnody is a major portion of Free Church worship which, since Isaac Watts's time, has come to regard as essential what it previously rejected as unscriptural. There is ample opportunity for creative selectivity from the wealth of Christian hymnody. Frequently, a church musician helps in selecting hymns that are both an integral part of a particular occasion and appropriate to the people's musical abilities.

A fifth possibility for creativity occurs in the provision of *musical and visual arts* for the occasion. Protestants are slowly beginning to realise that if each Sunday is a unique occasion, the visual character of the worship space should change each week to reflect this. We have long expected music (except service music) to vary weekly. Since mid-nineteenth century, choral music has come to play a major role in Free Church worship although a sound liturgical rationale for the presence of anthems never seems to have developed. Much choral music remains neither good nor bad but simply irrelevant to the occasion at hand, remaining the least integrated part of many services. Yet the potential for making it integral is present.

Banners have become legion since the mid 1960s. If nothing more, they give many people who are not singers a chance to offer their talents in the service of the worshipping community. Other visual arts are becoming more common: graphic arts, textile arts, photography, painting, and sculpture. At last a host of talents are being welcomed in churches that once had ears for music but no eyes for visual art. Thus the invitation to creativity has been extended far beyond the clergy.

3. THE BEST AND WORST OF LITURGICAL CREATIVITY

What can be learned from the worship experience of the Free Church tradition? What can be done to enhance such worship? What problems are endemic to this tradition and what gifts does it have to share with others?

A distinction must be made immediately between the *trained imagination and the untrained*. This is probably the chief problem for the Free Church tradition. Where a maximum of freedom is allowed, a maximum of training would seem requisite. Yet, unfortunately, the seminaries of denominations which worship according to the Free Church tradition have, hitherto, done very little to train future clergy in the possibilities available in worship. This is not a failure confined to the Free Church tradition but it has consequences that traditions using a service book can avoid by falling back on rubricism to enforce minimal standards.

One who has little or no training in worship is most likely to be captive to the familiar. He or she is not apt to have much opportunity to be creative without some knowledge of the history of Christian worship and a grounding in the theological foundations of it. One is free as long as one knows what is essential; without this knowledge one never dares stray too far from the sure and familiar. Liturgical knowledge, then, is a liberating discipline. The absence of it means captivity to the familiar. The Free Church tradition faces the challenge of developing liturgical scholarship and teaching resources in order to liberate its clergy.

For example, it is wonderful to be able to shape the eucharistic prayer to the time and place needed. But this is indeed perilous if one is unaware of what ought to be in such prayer. Without some criteria, one proclaims in such prayer a truncated faith. With such standards, it can be a magnificent bit of pastoral theology. In the absence of knowledge of its classical ingredients, one is vulnerable to the personal tastes of each individual pastor, edifying or not.

For the fullest expression of creativity to take place in the Free Church tradition, education is crucial. In its absence, worship in the Free Church tradition frequently becomes more hackneyed and stereotyped than in churches with fixed forms. An untrained pastor is not to be blamed; wells simply run dry when not replenished. Service books do, at least, provide options; the untrained imagination knows few.

Accordingly, at various times efforts have been made to give the minister what the *Westminster Directory* called 'some help and furniture'. The *Directory* is a book of rubrics which gives guidance for the ordering of worship and the creation of its various parts. A recent United Methodist publication, *Word and Table* (Abingdon 1980), is a similar attempt. The purpose of such volumes is to indicate essential constancy in Christian worship while encouraging diversity. One cannot utilise any portion of the Christian tradition unless one knows that part. Indeed, one is condemned to repeat history if unaware of it. Such volumes can be liberation manuals if seen as recitals of what has been regarded as essential in Christian worship. Only then can one shape these essential words and actions in ways appropriate to one's congregation. Some of the most creative services today are broadly but knowingly eclectic in utilising the best available materials from twenty centuries and two hundred nations for Christian worship.

Of course, not all can be anticipated in training. The unexpected possibilities of spontaneity have much in their favour. The Pentecostal tradition represents a break away from the Free Church and Methodist traditions of worship to allow precisely these possibilities. Yet even the Pentecostal tradition operates within certain assumptions, if not actual structures, in which spontaneity can happen. Paradoxically, some of the most fixed traditions have recently learned to accommodate themselves to spontaneity so as to have both the advantages of immediacy and yet a firm anchor.

A distinct advantage of the Free Church tradition is the immediate possibility it offers for remedying acts and words which come to be recognised as unjust to various persons. When it is perceived that certain words are demeaning or oppressive to members of the community, the words can immediately be changed. We have become increasingly aware of the dangers inherent in worship (as in any other public act) of reinforcing unjust attitudes. Once sensitive to an injustice in worship, the Free Church tradition need await no approval from authority or alteration of a service book to move towards justice. There is thus no need to perpetuate unjust structures in church or society through worship. The Free Church tradition frequently had led in eliminating language that demeans blacks or that suggests maleness is normative humanity. It has shown leadership opening in ministerial roles to women or in treating children as of equal value to those old enough to think analytically.

The creativity expressed in Free Church worship is basically a pastoral matter. At its best, it reflects faithfully the identity of the people who worship. This demands an intimate relationship between pastor and people; it is not the province of the visiting preacher. Of necessity, the pastor must know his or her people well. A fairly low clergy–laity ratio is necessary and often possible in the average Protestant congregation of about 350 people. One can know 350 people well, but not so likely a thousand. Beyond knowing them, one must be willing to accept them culturally as they are, not as one might wish them. The clerical culture that seminary inculcates in so many clergy is a real barrier here. This can be very painful especially in such areas as music. Seminary training inclines one to have certain standards of good taste and to wish to impose these on others. Some willingness to accept others' standards or lack of them is essential. This may be agonising for many clergy but possibilities for discrimination can be discovered at each level.

Finally, one must love one's people if one is to minister to them in creative fashion in the Free Church tradition. Nothing will be perceived as creative, no matter how original, without the clear sense that it is offered in loving service for others. After all, the worship is the congregation's own worship, not the clergy's masterpiece of creativity. One must know, accept, and love one's people for creativity to have any value in worship.

In the presence of knowing, accepting, and loving, Free Church worship has almost unlimited qualities for relevancy and authenticity in helping people express their worship in ways most appropriate and meaningful to them. This tradition offers both the best and the worst of possibilities for creativity in worship. It gives a pastor opportunities no other tradition can match; it also provides pitfalls no other tradition has as yet been willing to risk. Apparently the popularity of churches offering worship in this tradition in America, at least, is evidence that the values are worth all the risks involved.

PART III

Experiences Since Vatican II

Herman Wegman

Significant Effects of Insignificant Changes

THE TITLE of this article was provided by the editors. It is an interesting one, but it contains the danger of subjectivism. Who is to decide what are significant differences? Who is to judge whether a change in the ritual is small or not? I would not want to make such a judgment myself. In a spirit of chivalry, then, I am bound to admit in advance that the following lines have been written as the result of a purely personal assessment and that another author would undoubtedly have approached the subject from a different point of view. I have drawn conclusions from my own experience and from my own practice based on that experience. What follows is synchronistic and contains no historical details. I have chosen to describe four aspects of the celebration of the Eucharist.

1. THE USE OF SCRIPTURE

The Roman mode of celebrating the liturgy, which can be found in liturgical books that have been published since the Second Vatican Council, is characterised by a deep concern for the message that Scripture has for men and women of today. This, of course, involves a number of specific hermeneutic problems and every preacher has something to say about these. It should, however, be a cause of great rejoicing that Holy Scripture has been placed in the centre of the liturgy—the Roman liturgy has been considerably strengthened by this and the ecumenical thrust that has resulted from it has been world-wide. The Roman rite reflects a consciousness of the unique importance of the reading of Holy Scripture and the rites of the other churches are now characterised by a growing interest in the structured reading of the Bible following an annual cycle. The Roman lectionary for Sundays has therefore been echoed in the other churches as well as critised. It is recognisably present in several Protestant lectionaries.

A slight change has taken place with results that are not so slight. I am referring here to the book used in the liturgy, the edition used by the reader. Generally speaking, a lectionary is employed in the Roman rite. This consists fundamentally of an anthology from the Bible containing the 'pericopes' provided for each particular day. The readings in such a lectionary are ready-made for reading aloud. A complete missal or *missal plenum* is no longer used. Its place has now been taken by a book of prayers or sacramentary and a book of readings. It is, however, worth mentioning in this context that frequent use is made of a complete edition of the Bible instead of a book of pericopes.

We should be careful, however, not to dismiss this practice lightly by attributing it to the influence of Protestantism. This may well be true, but it tells us nothing about the background to the choice of the Bible for use in the liturgy, that is, a complete edition containing both the Old and the New Testaments. To introduce a historical note at this point, we are bound to recognise that this usage is not Protestant in origin—it goes back to the earliest liturgical tradition, in which pericopes and lists of pericopes from the Bible were used. I employ this method myself at the moment and am reading the Bible with the help of lists of pericopes which have been composed to cover a fairly long period.

What then, is significant in this slight adaptation in the ritual, that is, the use of the Bible in the liturgy? I believe that it points to a different view of Scripture and a different experience of the liturgy. In the eastern and the western or Roman liturgies, there has always been a preference for a typological reading of Scripture, a concordant reading of the Old and New Testaments, in which—and this is the essential aspect of this way of reading Scripture—the New Testament is seen as the fulfilment of the Old. The Gospel is the heart of the matter and the New Testament is the basis of the liturgy, which is a celebration of faith in Jesus, the anointed one of God. The Old Testament reading proves the correctness of the reading from the New Testament and makes God's saving action in Jesus of Nazareth clear and at the same time brings it to fulfilment.

The new Roman lectionary is built up with this in mind. The Gospels are read completely or more or less completely in three years on Sundays, but the short readings from the Old Testament are chosen in such a way that there is a harmony or counterpoint, but at the same time so that the Old Testament is always orientated towards the New. We are therefore bound to say that the Old Testament is not expressed as such. It appears in the liturgy as a kind of prophecy of what happens in Jesus' life.

This, then, is one view of Scripture and public worship, one might say the traditional view, but it is not the only possible one. We now have a better understanding of the Bible, the Jewish tradition and biblical exegesis and this means that there is another possible way of reading the Old Testament, which may perhaps be more obvious, certainly if we look at it from the point of view of the Protestant tradition of reading the Bible.

If we use the Bible rather than a lectionary in the Sunday liturgy, we are in fact showing that we want to move in a different direction in our understanding and our carrying out of worship. To summarise this intended change of direction, we can say that we want to give an equal and independent place to both the Old and the New Testaments. In practice, this means that we do not want to cut the Old Testament up into little pieces and stick the pieces on to the readings from the Gospel, but that we prefer to read it as an expression of God's covenant with his people in its own right.

The use of the Bible in the liturgy in this way, then, is, in my opinion, a hermeneutic theological choice and has everything to do with the present self-understanding and self-knowledge of Christians and the way in which that self-understanding has determined the type of liturgy. Let us briefly look at this self-understanding, first from the negative point of view and then from a more positive standpoint.

A negative description shows that this modern Christian self-understanding is different from that which underlies the Roman liturgy, which is based above all on an unchanging Christian self-consciousness, in which the Old Testament is seen as the 'history of the Jewish people' who rejected the Messiah and can consequently only be considered as a 'preliminary step'. It can in fact, according to this view, only be properly understood in the light of the New Testament, that is, by Christians who have received, in Jesus, the only truth. To this one truth men have to be converted. In this Christian self-consciousness, it is also possible to adhere to the fact that the future and the kingdom of God will be the fulfilment of what is already present here and now in the Church of Jesus in a toned down and muted form. The outline of the kingdom of God is, however, already present in the Church.

In the light of this self-understanding, the Christian churches have, since the earliest times, seen themselves as placed in sharp contrast to the pagans and unbelievers and, at certain times especially, to the Jews. Salvation can, in this self-understanding, only be found in conversion to the Gospel and to the place in which that Gospel is read aloud—the true Church of Jesus Christ is the only way to salvation.

A more positive approach is, however, also possible. On the basis of the witness borne by the New Testament itself, a more modest Christian understanding is undoubtedly also more appropriate. I cannot go into this positive appreciation of the Christian self-understanding in detail here, but would point, for example, to the fact that, in Jesus' own view (as described by the first Christian communities), the Torah was not abolished. Jesus himself said that he was on the way of the Torah and that he was experiencing the Torah in a way that was new to his contemporaries (although it was not new in itself). In other words, he experienced the Torah not legalistically, but as a way of life and as an expression of the covenant between God and men and between men and God.

In his letter to the Christians of Rome, Paul struggled with the identity of the message about Jesus Christ, through whom 'we have peace with God' (Rom. 5:1). What, then, is the situation with regard to God's faithfulness to the covenant with his people? This is surely a very incisive theological problem! What is in any case quite certain is that Israel was not in any way written off, but continued to be the stock on to which the Christian message is grafted. There can be no question of Christians overestimating their own importance (11:25-26). That is why the New Testament is not so new that the Old is written off. We may even ask ourselves whether it is right to speak of an Old and a New Testament!

Viewed in this way, the use of the Bible in the liturgy—reading from the Torah, the prophets, the Gospel and the epistles as independent witnesses to the covenant—is a radical 'manoeuvre' or an adjustment of theology about the Christian Church and its liturgy to more relative proportions. Together with Israel, the community of Jesus Christ is also striving to establish the signs of the kingdom of God in this world. The Church, then, is a church with the churches, a community with Israel, on the way to the coming kingdom of God.

2. THE BREAKING OF THE BREAD

The breaking of the bread in the celebration of the Eucharist is a gesture that has been neglected for a very long time. It has also been reduced to a clerical rite, since only the bread of the one who is leading the liturgy is broken. A piece of the bread is also dipped in the wine, which is drunk only by the same president of the celebration. The breaking of the bread represents nothing in the present rite and only the *Agnus Dei* provides any emphasis. And yet the breaking of the bread is called an essential rite in the celebration of the Eucharist. Very many communities have become aware of this anomaly with, as a consequence, a change in the rite. Wafer-thin hosts have been abandoned and firmer, more solid 'wheaten' hosts have come to be used.

On the other hand, a distinction is still regrettably often made between the large host

E

which the priest shows during the consecration and the smaller hosts given to the people. In the sort of practice that I am aquainted with, this distinction is, it is true, no longer made. There is a bowl with hosts of equal size and these are broken and distributed among the people. The breaking of the bread has become a community-forming gesture—the bread is offered or handed on after the participants have broken it with and for each other. This is a small ritual change, but its consequences are not so small.

The biblical concept of breaking the bread has in this way been restored to a position of honour and this means that the celebration of the Eucharist by the community has been, as it were, made subject to this gesture, which goes back to Jesus himself, who gave us the task of doing what he had done and to do it in remembrance of him. This small ritual change has made it possible for the participants to experience the Eucharist as a gesture of breaking and sharing with each other as a way of emphasising the words of blessing addressed to God. The gesture signifies—is a sign of—the multiplication of the loaves: in the desert, the small amount of bread was broken and shared and through this gesture the bread became a large amount—twelve baskets full. A miracle of sharing and feeding.

The breaking of the bread also makes the Eucharist a critical event, rather than what it so often was in the past—an uncommitted participation in a sacrament given by God. By breaking the bread, we show that we cannot and will not participate unless we have shared and distributed the gifts that we have received from God. This, too, is a sign of the attitude of those taking part, that they want to live in the spirit of what is done ritually in the Eucharist.

The breaking and sharing of the bread are a sign, then, of what all who do it want to make into a living reality—a just world, in which everything that is due to everybody is shared. In the desert world (a desert made for the most part by western hands—hands which grasp everything for themselves), the breaking of the bread is a gesture of conversion and of a change of 'normal' human behaviour. The participants in this gesture take bread, but do not eat it, until they know that all men and women have enough to eat. The breaking of the bread prevents us from simply celebrating the Eucharist or from reducing this sacrament to the level of a purely personal and inner event of grace. The sacrament becomes a sign of incredibility if it is not accompanied by this gesture of breaking bread and does not signify a conversion. This rite may be a small one, but I am convinced that its restoration will have great consequences for our experience of the Lord's Supper.

3. THE WAY OF RECEIVING COMMUNION

It is difficult to ascertain precisely how and where it began and it might be an interesting and worthwhile piece of contemporary history if it were written. What is certain, however, is that, during the period when the liturgy was being renewed in the late 1960s in the Netherlands, it suddenly became a common practice to give the people communion not on the tongue, but in the hand. There were, of course, reactions of alarm because a sacred event was being desacralised and sacred gifts were being defiled, but it was not long before the new practice was accepted. Hygienic reasons were suggested, but it was human reasons that led finally to the definitive breakthrough of the new rite. It spoke to men much more fully precisely as men. People felt that they were no longer being fed with sacred and untouchable gifts by the sacred hands of a consecrated and exalted person. This new way of receiving communion gave them the feeling that they were being addressed as fully human beings who were capable of acting.

This apparently slight change in the rite at once meant that a liturgy that had so far been at least to some extent alienating came much closer to those who were taking part. Receiving communion became a human action and the gesture of receiving in the hand made a more close participation possible. I know well from my own experience how this different way of receiving communion rapidly gained ground in the Netherlands. Dutch people on holiday abroad were astonished that it was not done elsewhere.

Putting out one's hand to receive communion proved to be almost a challenging gesture—a form of 'Hollanditis' in the Roman Catholic Church. Later, of course, it was accepted into the Roman rite and at the same time also ritualised, certainly when the newness of the gesture wore off and its value had evaporated. The fact is that rituals are so easily carried out in a ritualistic manner. The bread has also come to be distributed very quickly once again, sometimes even beating the record set before the Second Vatican Council.

This way of receiving communion has a variant. The manner of receiving 'communion in the hand' is, in other words, varied by taking it out of the bowl or dish which is offered by the president or handed on from one person to another. This is a gesture of taking rather than of receiving. It is sometimes combined with breaking the bread, as described above. The bread is broken for the next person, to whom it is given. This small alternative gesture has effects that are not so small. Let us briefly consider them.

What is most striking about it is that taking the bread is parallel to taking the cup, a gesture that is, for practical reasons, which are not really justified, seriously neglected in the Roman Catholic Church (often with an appeal to a now out-of-date theological principle that Christ is received totally in the bread alone). Together, the rites of taking the bread and taking the cup are in accordance with the rites of the meal as described in the Gospels and especially in the amount of the institution of the Eucharist. They clearly form the basis of the Eucharist itself: 'He took the bread . . . and said: "Take and eat". . . .'

Jesus himself almost automatically practised the Jewish rite of the meal, which included not only the prayer, but also the breaking of the bread and the handing on of that broken bread to the companions at table. One person, then, leads in prayer and gesture, but he leads in a shared meal, in which all those present are equal. The rites determine the togetherness of the partcipants in the meal and at the same time they draw attention to their distinctive qualities. The gesture does not presuppose a mass of people—on the contrary, it goes against this. Each individual is invited to 'set to' and take the bread and the cup. Taking the bread is giving consent, agreeing to participate in the meal. This way of taking communion, then, is a distinctive gesture in which each person himself or herself acts, in taking the bread that is offered on the dish and handing it on. There is no question of receiving as an insignificant person the sacred gift of the Holy One. Each person is, on the contrary, invited to take part. It is possible to apply a frequently used word in this context and say that the gesture is democratic. It has been employed for a long time in the Protestant rites, possibly in reaction to the Roman rite.

The effects of this small change are quite significant. In the first place, the Eucharist ceases to be a sacred event and becomes the celebration of a meal shared with others, to which all are invited individually by the Lord. The taking of the bread is a personal act of participation and of acceptance of the invitation. Especially in the handing on of the bread, the gesture is also a sign of togetherness. Finally, this variant in the manner of receiving communion is also important in that the part played by the one leading the celebration is relativised. He gives the dish, letting go of it so that it can be handed on from one participant to the next. In other words, he lets each person share in the role of sharing with others. He is also the last to take bread from the dish, which is handed back to him by one of the participants. Experience has proved that this way of 'receiving' communion, combined with the gesture of breaking bread, changes the 'image' of the Eucharist and the experience of the sacrament.

4. GREATER SIMPLICITY

I do not intend to describe the order of service in detail here. All that I shall do is to draw attention to a number of small ritual details which can be included under the heading of 'greater simplicity' and which have a significant effect.

Liturgical vestments have undoubtedly become much simpler and are, moreover, now worn by fewer people. There are no more directly liturgical assistants. The one who is presiding over the liturgy leads in prayer and preaching and, for the rest, he is usually helped by people from the community. Someone comes forward to read from Scripture, the bidding prayers are said in a suitable place in the church, the gifts are brought up and there is a collection (a gesture that gives credibility to the breaking of the bread). There are no ranks and the liturgy is not determined by a hierarchical principle. Ritual gestures are reduced to a minimum, so that full justice can be done to the essential rites and gestures. There is no attempt to carry out a precise ritual as perfectly and as accurately as possible. The 'rubrics' and the 'stage-management' are only means, not ends.

I cannot avoid a brief historical note if I am to draw attention to the reason for and the intention of this greater simplicity in the liturgy. If the 1970 missal is studied carefully, it soon becomes clear that the rubrics of the ritual of the mass are still those of a ritual intended for a cathedral. The rite itself is much more translucent and there is provision for participation by the believers present, but the outlook is still very exalted. The one presiding over the liturgy may be a priest, but the way in which he is treated in the rubrics and expected to act according to those rubrics makes him a *sacerdos*-bishop. The priest is the undisputed leader and the others present have all to be gathered around him. The ritual, in other words, goes back to the liturgy of the Bishop of Rome, although it is reduced in size and splendour for use in parishes. It still has a hierarchical aspect and 'imperial' characteristics.

What is more, this still distinctively Roman ritual also has clear sacral aspects. The washing of hands, the emphasis on the style of the celebration and the types of vessels and other objects used, the rules to which the participants are still bound and the exclusion of certain categories of participant (notably women)—all these details remove the rite from the confines of time and space and raise it up into exalted spheres, a sacral environment which can only be entered by one who has been ordained.

I have perhaps been a little excessive in my description of this Roman rite for the sake of clarity, but fortunately it has been attacked, changed and simplified. A Christian community cannot celebrate a cathedral liturgy, an ordinary church is not a cathedral and the leader in the celebration is not a bishop. The sacral sphere of the Roman rite does not encourage Church emancipation and human development. This does not mean that there is no emphasis on style any longer in our churches (are we, who are not bishops, not capable of acting with style?), but it does mean that the style is adapted to the situation, to our own time and place and to people living here and now. A simpler, more austere form of liturgy is something for which many people today can feel great empathy. It is more open to many who are seeking. It invites people to join in and there is no sacral threshold to cross.

I may perhaps have shown by means of a few examples drawn from the liturgy of the Eucharist that insignificant changes may be very significant in their effects.

Translated by David Smith

Anselme Sanon

Cultural Rooting of the Liturgy in Africa Since Vatican II

THE CELEBRATION of Palm Sunday leads our thoughts towards the picturesque scene of the Messianic entry Jesus made into Jerusalem, which he was to leave again with his cross in order to be crucified. Jesus certainly realises a prophecy (Matt. 21:1-12; Zech. 9:9) richly symbolic of humanity and gentleness in majesty.

In fact, we see the Lord escorted by the crowd and mounted on a young ass or she-ass. To those who ask why such a gesture, the reply is given: 'The Lord has need of them, and he will send them immediately.'

I have picked out this episode because it speaks: it is an evangelical liturgy in its simplicity and humility. Yesterday the Lord in the land of his own ancestors had certain natural human needs (such as drinking, when the woman had drawn up the water from the well in a bucket (John 4:7), sleeping, travelling by ass or by boat, going to the feast). He used these humble realities of our earth, of his earth, to live the evangelical liturgy, in order to lead his people as a good shepherd towards green pastures.

Are not many passages of the Gospel which are interpreted today as scenes or scientifically analysed parables, in the first place liturgies, celebrated in oral-style liturgy, such as the annunciation, the visitation, the announcing of the birth of John the Baptist, the Magnificat, the Benedictus, the presentation in the temple, the ascension, etc? These are liturgies, i.e., actions, gestures and attitudes celebrated in an oral milieu: these are true pastoral liturgies where the people act and understand on the basis of what they have, to be led towards what they must be before him who Is.

Did not Vatican II portend such a trend when it got down to the reform of the liturgy, or rather of the ceremonies and rites of the Roman liturgy? A great hope entered the hearts of us students, as we were at the time: for theology, dogma, doctrine, catechesis, hierarchical order, all that was very nice for the experts, but can the liturgy be liturgy without being given to the people of God? Are sophisticated ceremonies in expert clerical hands seriously liturgy?

Without expanding on these questions which haunt us almost constantly when we see how the holy liturgy is celebrated in our own diocese and elsewhere in other continents, let us take a look at the rooting of this liturgy in African countries since Vatican II.

What projects could be encouraged, guided by what principles, and what obstacles have opposed or stimulated them? This will be the main structure of our analysis.

61

1. WHAT IS THE SITUATION?

Even if it takes ten years to apply the conciliar texts on the liturgy, we shall take the time—such was the sentiment among several African bishops on liturgical reform since Vatican II.

That was in 1964 . . . and fifteen years passed—soon it will be twenty years. The situation is not far from that prevailing at the time of the christological quarrels of the fourth century: but this time it bears on liturgical quarrels, so strong are the feelings involved, though these feelings are often not very clear.

If the principles were so objective, why do they vary from one diocesan church to another? And if we are in a field which admits variations in the name of life, why argue about it? That all leads to minor irritations, insecurity, engendering a situation of liturgical stagnation: the bishops are not happy because the liturgy is not always celebrated as they would like; the people are worried because the new liturgy is not always familiar to them, the celebrant who wishes to nourish his congregation often leaves them hungry after the celebration.

What we have now are rootless, floating liturgies, for while everyone uses the word 'liturgy', some are thinking of ceremony, others of ritual, etc. . . .

I myself believe that there is a real liturgical hunger in the Catholic churches today: can one anywhere in the world draw sustenance in this from blanket prescriptions such as those issued by doctors, which are going to lay down the great avenues which Vatican II began to map out to lead us to green pastures?

The African communities, which are oral in style, very often feel near to the Gospel, which was given in an oral culture. And so they are led off course when attempts are made to govern them with a bookish liturgy, as though the religion of the Bible implied a religion of the book and a liturgy of the book! But no—the Bible is the Word of God handed down in writing, we are a religion of the Word and not of the book, so why impose on ourselves a liturgy of the book?

2. STEP BY STEP IN THE COMMUNITIES

The enthusiasm since Vatican II called for a new way of 'saying mass' and of 'giving the sacraments'.

The time of concessions granted by way of indults to the mission territories seemed over, since the new liturgy initiated what had previously been obtained only by means of applications to Rome.

The implementing decrees of February 1965 surprised more than one church by their speed and their liberality. As written information takes longer to arrive than sound waves (radio and television), current opinion was aware of reforms which the pastors of communities were far from having understood.

An initial period of sensitisation was needed for the priests themselves: and so the national and diocesan liturgical commissions came into being. However, up to now some entire Churches have no national liturgical commissions or even a link with the catechetical commission.

But it is mainly documents coming from Rome, read via their French or English versions, which determined the practice of the priests or clergy and that of the religious communities.

In the African churches, the liturgical reform of Vatican II has consisted in passing from Latin to a western language.

The de-Latinisation of the liturgy has not initially involved the systematic utilisation of the local languages, but recourse to the languages of the missionaries, according to the linguistic zones (francophone, anglophone, etc.). For the people, this has not meant a very great difference, except for the Latin chant, which they were sorry to lose; in the eyes of the élites it was a betrayal of the sacred language of the Church.

Everywhere the problem has arisen of translation. The documents of the new liturgy have had to be translated into one or more local languages. This had already happened in catechesis but before that had been experienced in the para-liturgies; thus, for example, the prayer recited in the local language, then sung and concluded in Latin.

Henceforth the local language came into its own, so that an old woman could exclaim: 'Now God is speaking to us in our own language!' The Church no longer spoke in a sacred language that everyone tried to understand with the words of his mother tongue; it itself began to speak each of the mother tongues of its sons of the various ethnic groups.

Certainly linguistic diversity is not the lot of all the African countries; the fact remains, however, that several still often include dozens of spoken languages.

An effort at linguistic unification seemed imperative: states have rarely tried it, even less so the Churches.

In many dioceses or vast regions translators have set to work, without always having access to either the Latin or Greek texts, making do with the translations they have in western languages.

What should be translated? The biblical texts, certainly, and the other liturgical texts. But how should they be translated? Translators thought of the past, of their schoolboy or student versions. Avoid misinterpretations and meaningless phrases and track down wrong meanings, to find the exact word and above all the idea—these are the rules to follow. Some translations undertaken by the missionaries contained obscurities even in their version of the Lord's Prayer. Taken over and continued by the autochthonous peoples, these versions, which conform more to the spirit of the language, are often a brutal shock for the congregation.

How many have understood that a liturgical or catechetical translation, made to be spoken aloud in a congregation which is listening, obeys other laws than those for an exegetical translation, intended to be read.

Meanwhile documents poured in from Rome at short or long intervals. Those involved were still polishing up their text when a new document arrived that had to be translated. Adjustments were made later, after liturgical experiments.

In fact, priests or parishes received authorisation to undertake liturgical experiments in this or that field of the liturgy. The change from the old to the new liturgy was such that people expert in liturgical matters and quite well educated communities were required—two factors seldom found together.

Hence the experiments were often pursued according to the whim of the persons authorised to carry them out; which explains why the results of almost twenty years of postconciliar liturgy seem meagre and fragmented. The clearest gains can, however, be listed:

(a) Some fields where the African genius excels have made real progress: this holds mainly for liturgical chant.

Taken from the Latin canticles and motets, fashioned anew with their own words and melodies in the local languages, these composers have been able to achieve a real level of creativity.

There are many of these composers, and moreover among Africans it is difficult to find anyone unable to compose a canticle or psalm. The African priests, religious and nuns, and catechists, have emerged as excellent composers without special musical training.

The Mass of the Savanes in Upper Volta (1956) and that of the Piroguiers are the first two known compositions of African masses! The former adapted the Latin language and

Gregorian melody to the rhythm of Volta drums. Heard over twenty years later, in 1981, it makes younger generations smile. But at the time it was very daring.

The repertoire of African liturgical chant is enormous: unfortunately the diversity of languages and the difficulty in distributing productions of the best deprive many of the communities of these great riches.

(b) After the chant, the proclaimed word: western education of a scholastic type is mainly familiar with the written word, made to be read; this prose, which is different from poetry, needs a lot of punctuation and other written signs.

African cultures are of oral type: the word is created in order to be proclaimed and heard. Literary translations are difficult to understand and tire the congregation. This is why the preaching of the missionaries is less successful than that of the autochthonous priests, so long as they in their turn do not betray the genius of their language.

Communities in Chad and Upper Volta are on the point of succeeding in this utilisation of the spoken word. The results are surprising: neophytes, helped by the rhythm of the drums, retain whole passages of the Gospel, such as the Prologue, the beatitudes, the hymn to charity; and they repeat them as easily as the Lord's Prayer.

(c) A third gain: celebration. Many of our communities rediscover celebration. What difference do you make between saying the mass and celebrating it? Exactly the same as that which exists between noise and music.

For over twenty years I have seen priests saying mass in my baptismal church, filled with the faithful: today, before so many people, they celebrate it. To celebrate is to make present and alive to one another the mysteries which are celebrated, for those who are celebrating it.

The rite stops being 'ready to wear' or 'ready to eat' and becomes an instrument of communication and communion with a community which wishes to enter into the mystery of Christ. Our liturgies allow to be celebrated in church the faith, hope and charity which have risen so recently in certain regions.

(d) One incidental gain: gestures and attitudes. The celebration carried out well, going beyond a mere performance of a rite and certainly beyond a mere ritual act, calls for the participation, the setting in motion of the assembly. It is the whole assembly which celebrates, guided by the leader of the celebration, the priest in the case of sacramental acts.

The crowd which has become an assembly shows its participation by the formulas of dialogue, of adherence, of thanksgiving, proclaimed or sung; it also shows its adherence by the gestures and attitudes it makes: standing, kneeling, bowing the head, lifting hands and head towards heaven.

But above all it marks the rhythm of the drum which permeates it, dwells in it and moves it to create a harmony of gestures and gesticular attitudes: what is called dance.

Dancing begins with those who sing and clap their hands when a psalm demands it: they bow in accordance with the song they are executing. It continues for those in the entry procession, offertory or communion: instead of walking as though going about their own affairs, they advance like people going towards God; for 'the more you approach God, the further off he seems'. This is why everyone will take two steps forward and one backward.

The dance can be led by a separate group which translates by the rhythm of all its bodily attitudes the spirit dwelling within each in the assembly. The dancer dances possessed solely by the rhythm; and rhythm is a spark emanating from a fire: the spirit.

In general western dancing is dictated by melody and harmony; African dances tend rather to marry the rhythm to very varied development.

I should like to make a remark here: dance is a bodily expression of the spirit: and spirits vary, being to a greater or lesser degree of the earth and of blood. Rhythm in Africa is their dynamising and purifying element: the expert eye can tell very well if the dancer is dancing for the public, for a third person or simply turned towards the inner spirit inhabiting him. Without this inhabitation dance descends into bodily exhibitionism which wounds the modesty and *a fortiori* the soul of the believing community.

The Christian liturgy we have inherited has neither feet nor arms: it has tried to be from everywhere and succeeds in being from nowhere. In contact with African humanity it could gain in humanity and in redemption, if it is true that what is not assumed is not saved.

(*e*) An indispensable area: liturgical vocabulary. The first translators of passages from the Bible and especially of catechisms into local languages had to face a certain number of problems which Fr Jacques Dournes noted in another context: the problem of the translation which becomes a matter of converting one culture into another.

Western Christianity always has the example of Tertullian who, in fixing the Latin vocabulary, allowed it to come out of its infancy. Our young communities were at this stage.

Just read the following, for example: 'Yezu ta sakrama kopra: batème, confirmation, Ekaristi, ordo. . . .' Except for a couple of words, all the rest does sound somewhat Latin. . . .

What should be translated? How should it be translated? What should be kept of the biblical realities, what converted into images and realities of the country?

I can recall one particular problem: the parable of the vine in John 15: Jesus said: 'I am the vine' (= vine for producing wine) or 'I am the grape-vine' (= wild vine of the savannahs)? The second translation offers a better understanding of the image suggested by Jesus, but on the other hand the whole biblical symbolism of the vine is lost.

To give the communities a liturgical and catechetical vocabulary cannot be the task of a single translator nor of a single generation. Where effort is systematically guided, a new language is given to the faith of the baptised and even to the human community around it; languages are spurred on by a challenge: to translate the new realities of the Christian faith; and they reveal their hidden wealth and their vitality. De-Latinisation goes hand in hand with the rejection of western sonorities in favour of a vocabulary more in accordance with the genius of the languages: it is still the same doctrine, but received differently.

Having reached this point, the translators, helped by the whole community, are capable of a work of creation: the same phenomenon encountered with regard to songs and liturgical music is found here. We have some liturgical compositions which will not fade, as they are so inspired, both by biblical vigour and local tradition. What emerges here has sprung from what has matured.

(*f*) Scope for the new liturgy. In spite of the limited number of priests, where postconciliar liturgy has gone furthest beyond the expectations of the African soul is in concelebration. Since they have seen three priests together in liturgical celebration, the faithful have rejoiced: this is the Church-communion, this is the Church-family.

The places of worship so carefully built before the Council often seem too small: recently, for confirmations, the whole village community was there, Christians, catechumens, and their non-Christian brothers. The chapel was too small: a large tree offered us its shade.

The new African liturgy needs space for processions and gestures, for it is action (the Constitution on the Liturgy, § 2, says that the liturgy is the practical exercise of our redemption). And until new places of worship are built, it takes place in the open air, under the celestial vault.

Sacred furniture, sacred art, liturgical vestments and vessels are challenges for our young artists. Although there are still communities which import everything from elsewhere, the majority would like to see their own artists and architects arising in their midst. The imaginary and the symbolic of the Negro-African world is trying to raise itself to the level of the faith, to say in an African style and in African forms how God saves us in Jesus Christ alone.

Certainly the doors are open wide enough for the rooting of the Christian liturgy in the African cultures. The results, which until now have been feeble, scattered and disparate, mean that the African communities are still hungry.

Certain steps are indispensable for the progress of a truly Christian and African liturgy.

3. TO CREATE AN ORAL-STYLE LITURGY?

There is no African liturgy. There are no African liturgies: as far as we know, our English- and French-speaking sister-churches of Africa south of the Sahara refer us to liturgies which are to varying degrees improved ceremonies or ones adapted from the Roman liturgy, an echo of our own situation.

We have had some contact with Madagascan, Ethiopian, Zairan and Cameroon celebrations and with all the churches of West Africa. The Madagascan liturgies held our attention by their unity of action, of celebration; those of the Cameroons by the beauty of execution of the songs. Song there is, like in the Zairan Mass, a vital act of transmission of a message. 'Song here in itself is neither poetry nor music, but a tool of purely oral transmission, a rhythmo-pedagogic and rhythmo-catechetic recitation.'[1]

The Zairan Church is well known for its Zairan Mass which is a Zairan rite of the celebration of the Eucharist. The churches of the savannahs and even of the forests of West Africa are distinguished by the very marked rhythm of their songs and their percussion instruments (drum, balafos, etc.).

In all this, one tends to forget that the liturgy is not just the rite of the eucharistic celebration, even though this is its apex. One also forgets that the liturgy as such is vaster than the ceremonies bequeathed by the Roman liturgy, which has become a bookish, scholastic liturgy, somewhat fossilised in many of its aspects.

Can we hope for something from the entry of the African liturgy into the liturgy of the Catholic Church? In themselves the principles remain clear, but here, too, Africa could surprise the believing world and it is by no means sure that the new impetus it has initiated will not shatter many outdated features.

Let us note a few preliminaries to this new impetus. First, it is not enough to start from the principle of adaptation: this would be to stifle the creativity which so marked the communities of the primitive Church. It would be to close for the Holy Spirit many doors of the current of renewal: until now, moreover, there have been few experiments which have exhausted §§ 37 and 38-39 of the Constitution on the Liturgy. All the texts on the reform of the sacraments rest on these paragraphs.

When we reach No. 40, which introduces radical reform through the introduction of cultural elements, communities relying on their pastor prove doctrinally and psychologically unprepared. For example, there are cultural regions where only the dead receive food in the mouth, and yet people think that they cannot receive communion in the hand on the ground that touching the body of Christ is reserved for the priest.

The new Churches should be convinced of their duty of creativity, which implies that the bishops become fully aware of their freedom and responsibility in liturgical matters.

The era of improvisation can be ended at the whim of anyone, but not the duty to create, to invent, in the long and slow search for a new liturgy.

To hinder the young churches from creating could have serious consequences for their future and the future of the Church. Our feeling is that in the zones where the Roman liturgy has flourished, the communities have found it more difficult to resist pagan and Moslem invasions, unless they have made themselves evangelising, like the Mozarabic liturgy.

And so the principle of adaptation should be extended to achieve the creation of new liturgies, then to remind the bishops, in a spirit of expansion and not of restraint, of their duty and responsibility in liturgical matters. Finally, to allow the young churches to make of their celebrations not the execution of ceremonies but the celebration of their new faith and the instrument of evangelisation of their milieu.

Let us point out a few main features of this African contribution to the liturgy of the whole Church:

(a) Broken rhythm

From the very start, the African celebration in the liturgy breaks the law of the three unities: unity of place, time and theme. We know the liturgy does not celebrate ideas[2] or themes but facts and gestures: unfortunately, a bookish liturgy tends to forget this and it is loudly announced—at least in the languages of books coming from the West—that the theme of our celebration will be. . . .

Through its rhythm, African celebration is broken. It is of the type of initiatory celebrations which we know in the new ritual of baptism, and also for the stations of Lent of the old Roman liturgy; time is broken up, the place changes because one goes from one church to another, from one Sunday to another to encourage the communities and their catechumens.

It is in this way that the celebration of the festival of Christmas or Easter in our parish churches is repeated in each secondary church and in each village: the festival of Christmas is celebrated from one village to another until the beginning of Lent.

(b) Liturgy of participation

If such a liturgical celebration stretches out over a large area and a long period, it is because people are taking part in it: people march, sing, take part—one is a participant. The liturgy of our books would find it difficult to open such avenues to us: books recount what has been done, what is to be done, and the main celebrant comments on this to say in what spirit this was done and why we are going to do it.

The liturgy of the gesture has been lost and with it the profound laws of celebration, of all human celebration, i.e., repetition, dialogue, utterance.

Let us look at the liturgy of welcome at the beginning of eucharistic celebration. The officiating priest welcomes the congregation simply by saying: 'The Lord be with you.' The response is known. Then it continues with penitential preparation. Now we know that Jesus handled it differently (John 20:19-23).

The present celebration is a rite of welcome of the Risen Lord on Easter Day: Jesus enters, greets twice; three times he makes a gesture: showing his hands and his side, then breathes on them; he confides a message of peace, mission, the Holy Spirit. These gifts dictate the attitudes: the gift of the presence and peace call forth joy; then the mission and finally the forgiveness of sins.

There is only one theme: Jesus repeats it, each time going further.

(c) Liturgy as receiving

A third contribution of an African liturgy could be the liturgy of receiving and giving. The formula is well known, that of giving and receiving. It is western in structure.

In their celebration of life, societies with an oral tradition know that everything that is living receives.

The faithful have been taught too much to come to give to God: Sunday should be given to God, mass given to him, praise given to him. . . . Before giving to God, one should understand oneself as a gift received. We come to give thanks for the gift received. To give is the part of God and man is on the side of him who receives before giving thanks.

The African liturgies would be betraying nothing of the grace of God and of their cultural roots by being celebrations of receiving and giving back. The demonstrative, explosive form, the gestures of welcome and offertory, the approach to the mysteries by signs and symbols, can easily be inserted in the rhythm of a celebration of receiving and giving.

The liturgy of receiving and giving tends to place things straight away into the context of experience. One can say here of the time of liturgical celebration as of silence that it has value only through that with which it is filled. A celebration wholly in words will leave more or less enriching words; a celebration which resorts to images and symbols will allow the heart rather than the mind to open to avenues of images and symbols.

(d) Oral-style liturgy

Today the audio-visual element has become an adjunct of prayer appealing to a fundamental experience, that of listening in man when all is silence and the word contains all its wealth.

Ever since the time of Christ the advice has been not to indulge in endless repetitions; the point was reached of excluding repetition altogether. Was not this to forget that the only prayers which remain alive in man and thus make him live spiritually are those which he repeats?

It is odd that the periods which suspected scholars who only were such when together with their books (*doctus cum libro*), did not have the same distrust towards the officiating priest with his book (*officians cum libro*).

The great difference between the Roman liturgy and many other human and religious liturgies is that the Roman liturgy has become and still aims to become a liturgy of the book, a bookish liturgy. Instead of taking on the Word to celebrate it, the officiating priests bring it into the assembly like an unmilled grain, an unslaughtered lamb. As one celebrant said, it is left then for the cooking to proceed in the assembly.

The opposite remains just as true: since it is the book which governs everything, some meticulously prepare their liturgical menu and once they are in front of the assembly they act like Pilate towards what is written: 'What I have written, I have written.'

Preparation for liturgical celebration should allow the celebrant to be free with the written documents to free the life, the word. Unfortunately, the laws of human communication are rarely applied to liturgical celebration.

To conceive an oral-style liturgy can help a lot. The celebrant stands among the assembly with the responsibility of opening the granary and distributing to the assembly according to its capacity for participation.

Making himself present among the assembly, the celebrant wishes to make them enter into the experience of Jesus Christ at some moment or other of his salvific mystery.

The celebration proceeds according to three roles:

interlocutor,
locutor,
hearer.

In principle the public (the assembly), the officiant and God himself each in his own time and turn, assume one of the three roles. God speaks to his people and they listen in the name of dialogue, the people listen and also speak in their turn, the officiant speaks and listens, addressing God and the people alternately, in the name of their God.

Oral-style liturgy is auricular and ocular, one sees and one hears; it is word and gesture; it is movement and repose. In this the liturgy of the burning bush experienced by Moses, that of Eli on Mount Horeb, or even that of Isaiah and Zachariah in the Temple remain parameters in the tradition.

(e) Celebrations of the faith and not ceremonies

When the perspective of particular liturgies appears, certain people cry out against the danger of particularism which, according to them at any rate, goes against universality. What do they understand by Catholic universality if not very often a certain security, a type of religious insurance, of celebrations with no smell or taste, which are the liturgies of everywhere and always, ceremonies of nowhere.

Special liturgical celebration is only a corollary of the evangelisation of special peoples. If the movement of the Spirit takes the Apostles to Macedonia or even to the house of Cornelius (Acts 10), God reveals himself in a different place: and who could or would dare to hinder others from receiving baptism in the same spirit and praising it in their own way?

The liturgical message of the young churches in all freedom should be not to ensure the ceremonies but to celebrate faith, hope and charity. For us the law of celebration, to be orthodox, is triple in nature: *lex orandi, lex credendi, lex diligendi*: faith calls forth the prayer of hope; the two are nothing without charity.

Those who lead Christian celebrations in front of an immense crowd of which only the smallest fraction is Christian know something about this: what have the others come looking for? They expect of the Church in prayer good news, the Gospel of peace and truth about death, about baptism, about reconciliation, etc.

The liturgies of the young churches are not ceremonies of Christianised people but celebrations of a completely new, completely warm faith. In them the community says to itself and to the non-Christian milieu what it believes, what it hopes and what it loves of its God and of the world. This is why celebration in itself is an act of faith which confirms the proceeding of the rites.

May the universal Church accept that the liturgy, the liturgical experience has an age just as communities have. For young and new-born communities, young and new-born liturgies.

The more the experience of the new churches proves itself, the more it appears that the debate on universality is more a problem of culture than of faith. The majority of our communities, born in the nineteenth century from missionary activity, have the faith of the last century: a rather organic view of the Church, practice of devotions (chaplet, month of the rosary, first Friday to the Sacred Heart, etc. . . .). From the point of view of faith and zeal, impetus is a good thing. Certainly this faith should be clarified and consolidated and we are fully aware of that, especially where ancestral and family practices are concerned (ancestor worship and polygamy).

But is not the error of the young churches of Africa and Asia often that they bring in another culture? Instead of understanding the message in the universal languages of the modern world, they understand it in their mother tongue (Acts 2:8-10); this fact, which is evangelical and which should act in their favour, proves a handicap in their confidence in their majority. To prove our good ecclesial faith, to show that we want to share the same faith without shipwrecking it, we mutilate ourselves, we deprive ourselves of the power to understand and be understood by our brothers in the faith who do not have the same culture as ourselves.

This partial experience, including new liturgical services proper to our situation, clearly indicates that:

1. the African communities are beginning to experience the liturgy according to their temperament;
2. they wish to translate it and express it in their traditions if a creative scope is allowed them, broader than ritual;
3. in various ways valid realisations are appearing which show cultural elements integrated in Christian celebration;
4. but nowhere, to out knowledge, is there an organic development of a truly Christian and African liturgy; and
5. to root the liturgy in our cultures remains a vast field to be cultivated, as also the rooting of the Gospel in the same cultural traditions.

But this field is ripening . . . God be praised.

Translated by Della Couling

Notes

1. G. Baron *Marcel Jousse, Introduction à sa vie et à son oeuvre* (Tournai 1965) p. 124.
2. Hans Bernhard Meyer 'Temps et Liturgie: Remarques anthropologiques sur le Temps Liturgique *La Maison-Dieu* 148 (1982-1984) 31.

Paul Puthanangady

Inculturation of the Liturgy in India Since Vatican II

THE GREATEST problems of the Church have arisen from the interaction between the Gospel and cultures. In fact every important phase in the evangelising activity of the Church has been marked by a new expression of the Gospel in terms of the culture of the people who were evangelised. Now this encounter between the Gospel and culture has had two consequences: in the first place, it demanded of the Gospel the loss of its external form: the word of the Gospel was to be like the seed that falls into the folds and furrows of every new historical situation—a new culture, a new age, a new society and new religious conceptions and sensitivities.[1] There it had to die and rise to a new existence, and the sapling was to draw sustenance from the milieu, building itself up with the human and the religious elements present therein and wax strong in God's light. Here there could be no question of importing ready-made liturgies, theologies, Church-structures and faith formulas. In fact this was what had happened in the early Church. The disciples allowed the external forms in which their Jewish-Christian experience was expressed, to die in order to rise and then realise itself in numberless historical particularities. The beginning of this awareness and the crisis through which it has passed are reflected in such New Testament passages as Acts 15, Gal. 2, Acts 10 and John 4.

Secondly, in the very process of universalisation of the Gospel many hidden riches of the Gospel become manifest. The variety of structures and forms in which this same message can be expressed has revealed the true universality of the Gospel in the process of being deeply affected, challenged and enriched in its meeting with the various cultures.

The history of evangelisation is marked by the impact of the great cultures on the Gospel. The encounter of India with the Gospel ought to have given a new interpretation of the Gospel and as a consequence given rise to an authentic Indian expression of faith, worship and ecclesiastical organisation. Unfortunately, however, this has not been so and the Church we have today is a Church that has been transplanted in its long developed but alien cultural forms. The renewal of the Church in India demanded an urgent removal of this state of alienation. Hence the efforts of renewal emphasised inculturation especially with regard to liturgy in the immediate post-Vatican II period. Today after sixteen years of struggle we can look back and point out the main underlying trends of this movement as it evolved through the various stages

71

of growth and development and also make an assessment of the present stage of achievement in the realisation of this objective.

1. THE BEGINNING OF THE MOVEMENT TOWARDS AN AUTHENTIC INDIAN LITURGY

The problem of inculturation of worship is by no means new to India. This had occupied the interests of celebrated missionaries like De Nobili and others as far back as the seventeenth century.[2] But after Vatican II it has acquired an new interest and importance especially in the light of the directives for liturgical renewal laid down by the liturgical constitution *Sacrosanctum Concilium*. The Catholic Bishops' Conference of India in its general meeting held in Delhi in 1966, in order to plan and programme the implementation of the Council decisions, officially accepted inculturation as the guiding principle to be followed in fostering liturgical renewal in India and went as far as to lay down certain guidelines for action. An Episcopal Commission for Liturgy and a National Centre were set up in Bangalore in order to implement the programme of liturgical renewal including that of inculturation of liturgy.[3] These official organs have been in operation since 1966, striving to make Christian worship in India relevant to the culture and genius of the people. It was a process that took into consideration the directives of the Second Vatican Council, the theological principles of inculturation, the cultural reality of the country and the pastoral situation of the Christian communities. It by no means was an effort merely to replace rituals with rituals or to introduce cultural elements indiscriminately into Christian worship.

2. THE PRINCIPLES THAT UNDERLIE THE MOVEMENT

(a) The theological basis

Every liturgical celebration is the celebration of the local church. The mystery of Christ becomes visible through the cultural expressions of the community. It throws light on the concrete life-situation of the people. The process of inculturation should take into account these factors and formulate principles that can serve as guidelines all through the movement. In the liturgy the Christian tries to meet Christ. In India this meeting has meaning and effect only if it takes place in the context of an experience. This experience should have a special characteristic: it should lead humanity to the core of the reality. In other words, it is a means to deepen interiority. 'The goal of man's life is to realise the supreme state which is beyond all modalities and forms, which is indivisible and unimaginable, and one without second.'[4] In adapting liturgy to India this aspect of interiority must be kept in mind. The meditative element has a dominant role to play in an Indian liturgy. According to the Indian tradition, there are different means used to achieve this. In the first place abundant use is made of nature and natural phenomena. Besides using flowers and light in abundance, worship is very much connected to natural events like sunrise and sunset. It was through nature that the Vedic Indian arrived at communion with God. Another element that is dominant in acts of worship in India is what is known as *Bhakti*, loving devotion. This is expressed through special types of repetitive songs, called *bhajans*, name prayer (*namjapa*) or *keertans* (long, drawn out songs of praise), etc. Finally, we cannot think of adapting Christian worship to India without taking seriously into account the Indian Scriptures which are a very important source of religious inspiration in India. Hence an Indian liturgy should be deeply experiential, leading humanity to the core of its being where God dwells, through the use of signs that are appropriate and in accordance with the Indian religious genius. It would certainly require a positive approach to the Indian Scriptures if this process of inculturation of worship in India is to be complete. The Vedic sage found worship as the point of humanity's passage to the transcendent order; it was the unifying focus of all the universe and the door to the vision of the absolute reality.[5] Indian Christian worship should ultimately lead to the fulfilment of the eschatological longing of the Indian soul.

Together with this transcendental dimension, there is another aspect that should be taken into consideration when we deal with the problem of liturgical inculturation in India, namely, the socio-economic reality of the nation. Liturgy should enable us to build up a new earth and a new heaven in India. The horizontal dimension is not so clearly present in Hindu worship. This could be a specifically Christian contribution to India. The liturgical celebration in India should interpret the concrete human situation with its socio-economic and political aspects in order that the Gospel may truly affect the culture.[6] If in the case of confrontation with the vertical element of the Indian culture the Gospel is being affected by the religious reality, changing the external forms of worship by the introduction of symbols from the religious culture of India, in the case of its confrontation with the horizontal element or human situation, the same Gospel must change the external forms of injustice and oppression inherent in the socio-economic realities of India.

If liturgy is the supreme manifestation of the mystery of the Church and the most efficacious means of fulfilling her mission, if it is the fount from which all her power flows, and the summit towards which all her activities are directed (SC 10), it follows that the mission of the Church and inculturation which are carried out throughout the day in varying spheres should reach their culmination in the celebration of the liturgy in indigenous forms.[7] It is this basic principle that has been operative throughout the process of inculturation that has been taking place in India during the past sixteen years.

(b) Stages of implementation

The task of liturgical inculturation in India follows a phased programme thoroughly planned and gradually implemented. The first phase of it consisted in the efforts to create an Indian atmosphere of worship: gestures, postures, forms of homage, objects and elements, silence and interiority. In order to effect this, the Liturgical Commission prepared a document that contained twelve points of adaptation to be introduced into the liturgy of the Eucharist. These were approved by the Sacred Congregation for Divine Worship in April 1969.[8] Later on, the whole Order of the Mass was rearranged in order to integrate these twelve points of adaptation into the celebration in such a way as to lead to an orderly flow and harmony in the conducting of the liturgical action. Thus, an effort was initiated towards the evolution of an Order of the Mass for India.

The second stage of our movement towards an indigenous liturgy for India consisted of some major adaptations such as the composition of prayer formulas, including the eucharistic prayer, preparation of rituals for the celebration of the sacraments and the celebration of Indian festivals. An Indian anaphora was composed with a view to proclaim not only the marvels done by God in Israel, but also in India and in the whole world, taking into account the language and the manner of praying specific to India. The text of the anaphora was circulated for experimentation and comments and was proposed for approbation to the National Bishops' Conference in 1972. But it was not declared passed due to a dispute over the majority of votes required; hence it was not officially forwarded to the Sacred Congregation for Divine Worship. The work of adapting the sacramental rites has been undertaken by various subcommissions and is still going on in various parts of the country. The plan of adapting the Indian feasts has been implemented to some extent. Masses were composed for the celebration of certain religious feasts such as Divali,[9] Saraswati puja,[10] some social festivities like the harvest

F

festivals and national celebrations like Independence and Republic Day. A commission was also set up in order to work out a draft for an indigenised form of the Liturgy of the Hours.

The third stage of inculturation of liturgy in India was concerned with the use of the Scriptures of other religions in the Christian liturgy. In 1973 and 1974, the National Liturgical Centre published *pro manuscripto*—a collection of texts from the Scriptures of other religions for personal readings and meditation. It was also proposed as a possible text for the Office of Readings for the eventual Indian edition of the Liturgy of the Hours. In this collection, together with the biblical and patristic texts from the typical edition of the Liturgy of the Hours, an optional reading taken from the Hindu and other religious literature was introduced. It was, however, very strongly felt that the use of non-Christian literature in the liturgy needed further and deeper study and reflection. A research Seminar on non-biblical Scriptures was conducted in 1974 in which the question was thoroughly examined by scholars in various disciplines.[11] The pastoral proposals based on theological and liturgical reasons regarding the use of the non-biblical Scriptures in the Christian liturgy were submitted to the hierarchy for consideration and decision.

(c) Policy of implementation

The renewal of liturgy is not merely a change of rituals. It has also an ecclesial dimension. It is, therefore, necessary to take into account the ecclesial situation of India while proposing plans and projects for the renewal. The Church was fully conscious of the fact that there exist three different rites in this country: Roman Rite, Syro-Malabar Rite and Syro-Malankara Rite. Although all three of them have been existing in India for centuries, none of them reflects the cultural reality of the nation. In this sense we may say that they all need to be indigenised. Hence all the three rites are to take up the task of renewing their respective liturgies without sacrificing their identity and specific tradition, and at the same time work towards the creation of authentic Indian forms of worship. Perhaps in this process they might arrive at something common, since the human element or the cultural reality is the same for all in spite of their particular ecclesiastical traditions.

Besides the ritual differences, India is a country of great regional diversity. The plurality of Indian cultural and religious traditions demands that the indigenised liturgy not be rigidly uniform. Each region ought to develop its own forms of worship, thus working towards an authentic form of worship. This will result in the creation of liturgies in India that are pluriform, but at the same time having many elements in common, since there is a basic cultural unity in the country in spite of the differences of expressions.

Out efforts towards an authentic Indian liturgy have also an ecumenical dimension. The other Christian churches are also invited to work towards the evolution of an authentic Indian liturgy within their own ecclesial traditions. Thus the policy of liturgical inculturation is an all round ecclesial initiative in which the goal is not a uniform Indian liturgy, but an authentic Indian liturgy with a variety of forms and expressions, which can manifest fully the richness of the mystery of Christ within the one ecclesial confession and celebration of faith: Jesus Christ is the Lord.

The results that have been achieved vary from rite to rite, from region to region and from church to church. In the Roman rite, the celebration of the Indian Order of the Mass and prayer services using Indian forms of worship are taking place in religious communities and particular groups. In the North of India the pace of indigenisation is faster, and even parish masses are conducted using the indigenised form. In the Syro-Malabar rite, a rite for the indigenised Eucharist was drawn up and used experimentally in some dioceses and institutions. But the spirit of inculturation has already entered into worship of the Christian community. This can be seen from the widespread use of Indian forms of singing, postures and gestures, decorations and other external elements of worship in the traditional Roman and Oriental forms of worship. It becomes all the more evident in the para-liturgical celebrations and celebration of popular devotions. Inculturation of official liturgical acts still has to overcome some obstacles before it can become a normal manner of celebration.

(d) An evaluation

The Indian Church took up the challenge of Vatican II and launched its activities towards the creation of an authentic local church when it courageously initiated the process of liturgical inculturation. But, as is the case with every movement towards renewal, the implementation has to meet with favourable and unfavourable situations, and the result, necessarily, is a mixture of success and failures. In spite of all these circumstances, the movement has to go on and for this it is necessary to evaluate its strengths and weaknesses. There is one basic reality that concerns the Church in India which must not be forgotten in effecting this evaluation. Even though the Church in India is at present indigenous in its personnel, it is a Church that is, to a large extent, conditioned by the colonial mentality. As a result of this, even though it is capable of proposing courageous initiatives, when it comes to implementation, attitudes change, compromises are made and the movement meets with obstacles from the very sources from where the initiatives began at the planning stage. Hence the inculturation of liturgy with all its problems and difficulties cannot be interpreted by merely taking into account the so-called liturgical factor alone; it is necessary to assess it in the light of the whole ecclesial situation.

In the first place, we shall take note of some of the positive aspects of the movement towards inculturation. Wherever indigenised liturgy was introduced with appropriate instruction and initiation, the acceptance on the part of the people has been almost total. The experiential character of the celebration has touched the emotional life of the Christians to such an extent that faith has begun to become more and more meaningful. This is noticed in a special way in the widespread use of Indian forms of singing and performing homage during worship. Participants who have had an experience of the indigenised liturgical celebration attest that this way of worshipping has given them a better taste for prayer, a sense of belonging to the Church that is their own, has created a greater awareness of God's presence in their lives, a greater appreciation of the cultural heritage of the nation as a gift of the creator, a stronger commitment to the Gospel, a more profound sense of respect for people who belong to other religions and readiness to join them in the common quest for fullness and fulfilment, a more experiential awareness of the mysteries of Christian faith and a deep-felt need to live a more authentic Christian life.

Secondly, we shall also take into account the difficulties encountered on our journey towards the creation of an indigenised liturgy and analyse the reasons that lie behind them. One of the first reasons why some people find it difficult to accept the Indian form of Christian worship is the very method of evangelisation that has been followed in the past. It was based on a negative approach to non-Christian religions and it was identified with the acceptance of faith expressed in a particular cultural form. In our task of inculturation, there are many elements that we introduce which are in common with the manner of worship of non-Christians. This causes many emotional blocks even for the people who are intellectually convinced of the values of inculturation. Another problem that the movement has had to face is that of the uneven character of the Christian community in India. We have a very ancient traditional Christian community in the South, which traces back its Christian life to the apostolic times, and the recently formed

Christian communities that are generally found in the North. The process of inculturation is comparatively easy with the new churches while the ancient churches have to face the uphill task of liberating themselves from centuries of cultural alienation, which they do not even recognise as alienation. A third difficulty is the lack of proper catechesis. The new changes demand a change of attitude and understanding. This calls for an effective pastoral action on the part of bishops and priests and lay-leaders. In a highly institutionalised Church, as is the case especially with the traditional churches of the South where even religious instruction is institutionalised, to attempt an approach towards the new demands initiative and courage to depart from the traditional method. Many do not have this. Finally the problem of implementing inculturation is not an isolated one. It is related to the whole problem of renewal. It is an undeniable fact that there is a general apathy towards inculturation and renewal today; there is a tendency to retain the *status quo*. Implementation of inculturation can never thrive in such a climate because it is a call to continue the renewal in a radical manner.

CONCLUSION

The Church is a mystery that happens; it is the continued actualisation of the Christ event in a place, within a culture, in the midst of a people. The Christian experience is authentic only in the measure in which it is expressed through the cultural manifestation of the place and the people. An indigenised liturgy in India will show that the Christ event is still happening in this country. It will be a sure sign that the Christians of this country can share their Christian experience with their contemporaries in a relevant and meaningful manner. It will indicate that the Church in India is living the mystery of Christ in communion with their brothers and sisters all over the world, manifesting its richness and beauty in their own particular way and thus contributing to the Christian heritage and universal communion.

Notes

1. S. Rayan 'Flesh of India's Flesh' *Jeevadhara* 33 (1976) 262.
2. S. Rajamanickam SJ *The First Oriental Scholar* (Madras 1967) pp. 54ff.
3. *Report of the General Meeting of the Catholic Bishops' Conference of India*, Delhi, 13-20 October 1966, pp. 11-17.
4. Mrdananda 'Worship in Hinduism' *Jeevadhara* 12 (1972) 519.
5. *Rigveda* I, 64.
6. *The Indian Church in the Struggle for a New Society* ed. D. S. Amalorpavadass (Bangalore 1981) pp. 66ff.
7. D. S. Amalorpavadass *Gospel and culture* (Bangalore 1978) p. 50.
8. *Notitiae* 48 (1969) pp. 365-374. The twelve points of adaptation approved by Rome are the following:

(1) The posture during Mass, both for the priests and the faithful may be adapted to local usage, that is sitting on the floor, standing and the like; footwear may be removed also.
(2) Genuflections may be replaced by the profound bow with the *anjali hasta*.
(3) A *panchanga pranam* by both priests and faithful can take place before the liturgy of the Word, as part of the penitential rite, and at the conclusion of anaphora.
(4) Kissing of objects may be adapted to local custom, that is, touching the object with one's fingers or palm of one's hand and bringing the hands to one's eyes or forehead.

(5) The kiss of peace could be given by the exchange of the *anjali hasta* and/or the placing of the hands of the giver between the hands of the recipient.

(6) Incense could be made more use of in liturgical services. The receptacle could be the simple incense bowl with handle.

(7) The vestments could be simplified. A single tunic-type chasuble with a stole (*angavastra*) could replace the traditional vestments of the Roman rite. Samples of this change are to be forwarded to the *Concilium*.

(8) The corporal should be replaced by a tray (*thali* or *thambola thattu*) of fitting material.

(9) Oil lamps could be used instead of candles.

(10) The preparatory rite of the Mass may include:

(*a*) presentation of gifts;
(*b*) the welcome of the celebrant in an Indian way, e.g., with a single *arati*, washing of hands, etc.;
(*c*) the lighting of the lamp; and
(*d*) the greeting of peace among the faithful in sign of mutual reconciliation.

(11) In the 'Oration fidelium' some spontaneity may be permitted both with regard to its structure and the formulation of the intentions. The universal aspect of the Church, however, should not be left in oblivion.

(12) In the offertory rite, and at the conclusion of the anaphora the Indian form of worship may be integrated, that is, double or triple *arati* of flowers and/or incense and/or light.

9. *Divali* is the Indian feast of lights celebrated after the great rainy season of Monsoon.
10. *Saraswati puja* is the Hindu feast in honour of the goddess wisdom.
11. D. S. Amalorpavadass *Research Seminar on Non-Biblical Scriptures* (Bangalore 1974).

Francis Sullivan

Psalm Translation: Creating a New Poem

I WAS asked to make English poems out of psalms. Those who asked me are convinced that most translations in contemporary English are not poetic enough. They think that if a contemporary poet/theologian is given a basic translation of a literal character, he or she—myself in this case—will be able to recover the psalm through a new act of poetic creation. The new poem is to work in a paradoxical way; its quality as an artwork in contemporary English will provide the spiritual experience of relationship with God which the original artwork intended, though the new poem is related to the old as art to art, not as mirror to face. Another purpose is to be served: the new poem made of the old one will create a further spiritual experience by expanding the scope of the original to include the contemporary without violating the integrity of either. It is a contemporary person who uses psalms as the expression of his or her soul to God or as the voice of God back. It is also a contemporary liturgist, composer, preacher, lector, who will be conditioned by a creative translation. Different styles provoke different responses because styles are metaphors in their own right. The people who want the poetry of psalms intensified in English clearly believe that the aesthetic experience is the spiritual experience. They do not accept a separation between an expression and an experience. They want the unity restored so that it is the psalm which provides the relationship to God, world and self, not the occasion of the psalm.[1]

I agreed to try doing what people asked me as a poet and a theologian.[2] What moved me to accept was the belief I also have that the aesthetic beauty of certain religious expressions is the truth of those expressions. Now, some time later, I have been asked to say what consciousness I have come to about recreating psalms into modern poems so that I might serve as a case study in success or failure for those who are convinced that the beauty of a psalm is the source of its spiritual meaning, and therefore the beauty of a translation is the one way to make a psalm's spiritual truth available to a community of belief. Understand the word beauty to mean what several traditions say it means, a charming material, like a human face, which creates its own space, draws us into communion with its own transcendence, and looks back at us for our good and our freedom.[3] The charism of beauty is its ability to create freedom in relationship, and to refuse owning or being owned, as in idolatries.[4] The relationship is iconic, as in Rublev's *Holy Trinity*, or in Chagall's *White Crucifixion*, or in Orozco's *El Hombre de Fuego*.

1. THE LYRIC IMAGINATION AND THE PSALMS

Half-way through my project, I know I can do about eighty psalms of the 150. These eighty engage my imagination sympathetically so that I want to make them modern English poems.[5] Some among them have great lyric play, some remarkable narrative intensity, some are profoundly confessional or didactic through imagery, some have feeling levels that are intricate and dignified in every human sense: they have a taste for a creating God, redeeming God, which is strong and lasting. The psalms I cannot approach are the ones that make my imagination powerless. Some require of the beauty of God or of the earth that they serve to destroy that which is against God or the earth. Some manifest the ugliness of revenge, the ugliness of cursing, some the narrowness of bigotry, some are exercises in hatred or exclusiveness.

These latter render my imagination powerless poetically and theologically because I work as a lyric poet and I have to feel at one with what I say. I cannot simply provide a source of language for feelings I cannot live without ruining my aesthetic hope. I have tried; I sense the loss, or I have it pointed out to me. I also work as a theologian who sees God as creator and redeemer, not destroyer and damner. I do not believe what I say if I translate lines claiming that God causes this or that slaughter for this or that good reason. Again, I have tried; I sense my insincerity, or I have it pointed out to me. I think that a lyric imagination has to be like the Suffering Servant of Isaiah's songs, willing to transform destruction into creation if at all possible, or like the poet of Job who refuses to permit God or Job to curse each other and die.

Those psalms that celebrate creation and redemption almost ask of themselves to become modern poems. The modern lyric in English has had to face so much destruction and damnation in history that it chooses every means possible to counteract that history. I do not mean escapism. I mean the lyric's refusal to take part in destruction and damnation, its attempt to humanise the destroyers and to manifest a transcendence much like the transcendence of the Suffering Servant. Such psalms also ask to become part of modern theology. These days, theology can only handle the God of compassion and make sense. The God who causes or permits evil in order to produce good ruins belief especially in innocent victims and in those who absorb the experience of innocent victims into their own. Psalms that beg compassion or speak compassionately blend into modern consciousness readily and do not split the one who uses them into a Jekyll and Hyde.

There are mixed psalms, creative and redemptive in the beginning, destructive and damnational at the end. The lyric imagination works with wholes, its treatment of the finish of a psalm conditions its treatment of the start. A lyric imagination at work on translation sees where it is going with its first words, rhythms, images. Theological understanding is also anticipatory, it knows starts and finishes, often with the same immediacy as imagination. For my imagination, my mind, mixed type psalms are very difficult to handle, and I either have to transpose the damnational passages into allegory or not touch the whole psalm. I am describing what happens, not what I wish to happen. To repeat, my schooling in the modern lyric in English and in modern theologies of the compassionate God makes me trust the qualities of some psalms and mistrust the qualities of others. A different sort of imagination, a more dramatic one, might not experience the same divisions I do. The lyric imagination is not above the human condition. It is not the one innocent among the many guilty. It is more like a prayer for restoration for all the broken forms, coming from an accomplice in the breaking who wishes to be so no more.

2. FOUR TRANSLATIONS EXAMINED

Here is my version of Psalm 88:

You are my life,
God, over and over my life,
will you hear me
say it, will you understand it,
a living death
is all I lead, body and soul.
People treat me
already as the ghost I am.
I sprawl like a
battlefield corpse in a fresh grave,
you forget where
you buried it, you feel nothing.
You threw me here,
no light, no limit to this place,
but I feel you
raging at me, the weight of you
splitting me off
from friends; they think I am hateful.
You lock me in.
I lose sight of you in this hole.
O God, over
and over I try to reach you.
If you surprise
the dead, do they thank you for it?
Do they tell each
other below how kind you are?
How beautiful
in darkness or oblivion?
I beg you, God,
to let me be your morning praise.
Why is it you
refuse me, God, why turn your back?
Around, around
I go the torments before death.
There is nothing
left of me after your fury,
your rising tide
of it until I am alone,
nobody here
but myself and death for a friend.

I used Dahood's Anchor Bible translation as the basis for my poetic/theological decisions.[6] Though Dahood's English is poor, his sense of the poetic is rich; he uncovers imagery well and consistently. This psalm requires a sense of immediacy because death threatens the relationship. Immediacy requires direct address, compression, insistence, repeatedly. The image underlying all the language is that of the grave. It is an image kindred to 'Sheol' in the older translations, and to 'living burial' in descriptions of modern camps—concentration or gulag. It is kindred to the image of jail and of human plight in the ancient and modern senses. The image does three things at once: it works as itself in the psalm version; it echoes the traditional imagery of the underworld; it echoes the imagery of modern victims. I think it does this triple work modestly, i.e., the psalm does not conquer other experiences for itself, nor does it pretend to be a 'holier than thou' religious expression. Far greater suffering has been recorded in far greater poetry. There are split emotions throughout the psalm which result from the contradictory relationship: the God of life is seen as the God of death, the God of love as the God of hatred. The psalmist begs life and love from the source of death and hatred, hoping to argue that source back to life-giving and loving. All the images conspire to return the relationship to one of life and love. A short stammering style derives from the images and the feelings they express. I use a syllable count to each line, 4/8/4/8 throughout, letting the accent float, so there could be a dialectic of order/disorder on the sound level, and so there could be for readers and composers both an expectedness and unexpectedness to the lines. The words themselves are kept to as straight a sentence structure as possible, to mirror the undeviating intensity of focus and repetition in the psalmist's consciousness. The basic tone is one of powerful longing, longing for a relationship of love and life, not for pure safety apart and untouchable by any one. There is some bitterness, some anger playing through nearly all the lines, even some gallows humour. These elements do not overbear the basic tone. The psalm is through-composed in my version so the whole of it has to be used. Excerpting the lines will be a rupture of the psalm's integrity.[7]

Here is my version of Psalm 104:

God, you delight my soul!

You are noble and mine,
richly clothed in beauty
You made the sun your coat.
You pitched the tent, the sky,
made rooms to store water,
used clouds for a roadbed,
used wings, messenger winds
and servant tongues of fire.
You built the earth firmly
so it would not collapse,
made the sea a blanket
so it covered mountains.
Then from your thunder-voice
the water raced away,
to run hills, to find holes,
to fit in every place.
You drew lines for tides
so not to drown the land.
You sprang the torrents free
to tumble down gorges,
to water the cattle
and let the wild ass drink,
basins for all birdlife
and caucus ponds for crows.
You splash rain on the hills.
You store goods in the earth,
grow grass to feed livestock,
mow hay for the plow ox,
summon grain from the fields
and wine to fatten us,
to make us flush with health
and glow with bodily strength.

You water cedars you
planted in Lebanon,
cedars for nesting birds,
junipers for storks' nests.
You put wild goats on peaks,
badgers in cracks of rocks,
teach moons to wax and wane,
the sun where to go down.
You draw dusk, then darkness,
set wild beasts on the prowl,
lions eager for kill,
young beggars after God.
At daybreak they creep off,
they curl up in their lairs
while we walk to our fields
and hoe them until dusk.
Your deeds delight my soul!
Your genius making them,
such different creatures.
You are a sea teeming
with fish no one can count,
a shipwright, a maker
of monsters to play with.
You remain their keeper.
They want their food from you.
At feedtime they spot you,
they eat out of your hand!
If you renege, they die,
their spirits turn to clay.
When your genius sets out,
dead things sprout from the earth.
Your eyes can shake the ground,
your hand make hills erupt.
I hope I sing to you,
my God, my whole life long.
If you can hear me sing,
God, you will be my joy.
I hope sins will vanish
and evil disappear.

God, you delight my soul!

I think the psalm has to be done as a breathless narrative which shows its delight in God through its delight in language and imagery of the most sweeping kind. The psalmist becomes God, in fact, in order to see the exuberance of God at work in sustaining creation. So a reader or composer can grasp the exuberance of God only in the psalmist's prodigal narrative and imagery. The line structure is to a syllable count 6/6 throughout, again to give a substructure to the careering narrative. There are many lines which simply run over, one into the other. There are also lines which are short explosions of wonder. Both types of lines together create a sense of chaos and order in constant dialectic, and a sense that the divine creation works with the same dialectic as the physical elements of the poem. The act of poetic creation is the metaphor for the act of world creation, the ecstasy of the one reveals the ecstasy of the other. This psalm also must be used whole. I have shifted the destructive elements towards the end from the concrete to the abstract, hoping that the shift will retain some sense of the destructive wish while retaining also the creative bearing of the whole psalm. Otherwise those elements rip the whole poem apart.

Here is my version of Psalm 6:

You are angry at me.
You punish me.
Please stop, I am worn out.
Stand in my place.
I am hurt to the bone,
my soul a bruise.
Will you keep after me?
Change, please, cure me,
save me, you are not harsh.
Can a dead mouth
know what to sing for praise?
I cry myself
to sleep, no song, so tired,
my pillow damp.
I darken what I see,
deaden my heart.
I know my tears reach you.
Death has no hold.
You take these words from me.
You accept me.
You shake death loose from me.
You bury it.

I decided to let nothing disperse the intensity of the psalmist speaking to God without blinking or looking aside. I do not even spare the time to say God, the 'you' repeated is direct, first as a recognition of the one who is the source of the pain, then of the one who can take the pain away, then of the one who can listen to how bad the psalmist feels, then of the one who lifts the burden that caused the pain at the start. The relationship is unbroken throughout; it shifts as music shifts without pause from heaviness to lightness. God is revealed in the varying 'you' of the lines, especially in the last four where relief and love mount in the firm, declarative sentences. The last sentences are the reverse in feeling of the first two, though they have the same declarative structure. The verse lines again are set to a syllable count, 6/4 throughout, yet there is a constant interruption within the lines to show the struggle of the psalmist to figure out what is to come of this life and death crisis. I have understood the final lines in an allegorical sense to mean the same death that threatens in the earlier part of the poem. This way I can keep a consistency of imagery through the poem and use the image, at the end, as a reversal of itself.

In the last example I will use, I failed badly. It is the Samekh section of Psalm 119:

I hate fickle minds; I choose to love your law.
You defend me, you command me, I wait on you.
Clear off, you scum, and let me obey my God.
Shore up my life, you promised, or you shame my hope.
God, keep me on my feet so I respect your word.

Bury all renegades; they adore what is false.
You treat evil as scum, so I love your law.
My skin crawls in awe and fear at the way you judge.

Burton Raffel wrote me about it: 'This is perhaps the worst of the sequence—and when a poet of your calibre falls this flat . . . it's got to be what in law is called "a flaw in the inception".' He goes on to say: 'It's not the poet who so thinks, but someone else, some other part of you, maybe the theological side, maybe the public-priest side, I don't know. But I do know it's not the poet part of Francis Sullivan.' Raffel is my touchstone in all this work of making English-language poems of psalms. My imagination simply did not connect with this love-of-the-law psalm. I was not able to find an image in myself which would reveal the image of the law. The translation is therefore mainly a display of verbal facility which is neither poetry nor theology. It may be that the psalm itself is a headstrong thing in the original and refuses poetic treatment.

When the aesthetic basis is right, the poem is germinated from within its own means and it reveals its own spirituality. When the aesthetic basis is wrong, the work is germinated from outside itself and turns into propaganda. I have to say that several priests and theologians did praise this which I am calling a poetic failure. I do not want to call them or myself and Raffel into question. I want only to bring out again two difficulties a poet-translator of psalms must face: he or she must create a work of art out of material that piety and liturgical use consider sacred whether it is artistically presented or not: he or she must find critics who know when the aesthetic basis and the piety are one in the work and when they are not. People can use this failed poetic translation because they can bring to it what it does not seem to have. We all must do this with many different texts.[8] I began this essay by citing the problem that we must use translations of poetic texts that do not manifest well the nature of the original through the nature of the translation, and therefore we lose something essential from the original experience.[9] I am speaking of contemporary translations used in liturgical settings, not about translations, transformations, done by poets in original ways, which are attempts to revive the psalm tradition, used or not in liturgical assemblies.[10] I can conclude with a series of statements about the problem I was asked to resolve as a poet and theologian.

3. THE CREATOR IN THE COMMUNITY OF BELIEVERS

An act of creation presented to a community gives it an experience of spiritual freedom. Poetic creation is one way. It reveals a primary activity of God and a primary activity of humankind, as we believe in both. Poetic translations make privileged texts available in a new language as acts of creation. The aesthetic beauty of the translation shows a community that the spiritual truth it believes in occurs equally within its own tongue. Its own tongue is not a conqueror. It is a mate. This realisation gives to the community a chance to enter into an adult union with God, not an adolescent union fitfully obedient and disobedient. The union is one of eros. The charm of the medium, the poetic text, is erotic charm because it asks the whole of a self to give and receive a whole self, and yet the poetic text insists on retaining the difference between one beloved and another.[11] The poetic translation is not the poetic original. And yet they are mates in belief, in loss of faith, in recovery, in penitence, in desperate hope, in lyric ecstasy, in the love of creation and redemption.

Failure to renew an act of creation by another act leads to an experience of subjection in a community.[12] Union with God becomes one sided, non-erotic; it becomes extrinsic, and beauty becomes an idol to distract the soul from its emptiness towards God, beauty becomes the image of the split from God, the place of the satanic, not the image of transcendence and the defeat of isolation. The lesson is not learned that the poetry of revelation, in its original, in its translation, gets free of ownership, free of propaganda, free of sectarianism, free of institution, and serves thereby as a reminder that humankind is free in the face of God, and God is free in the face of humankind, so that the relationship between the two must be created all the time, never coerced. How both God and humankind treat the medium of relationship, the psalm, in this instance the psalm translation, has everything to do with their integrity. Psalms that beg God to destroy and damn the sinful are a rape of poetry, and therefore a rape of relationship. Psalms that order humankind to destroy in God's name are equally a rape of relationship. The psalmist has control of both human and divine voice. The translator comes next. Then the community which lives what it expresses, or tries to, though often it lives around what it expresses, praying a violence, living a peacefulness.

I sense that people who want poetic translations of poetic originals, psalms, have a definite spirituality in mind. They want a love of integrity of form. Integrity of form means that beauty cannot be lost without the loss of truth. The truth is creative and redemptive. It is not destructive by intent, nor is it damnational. The passion, death, and resurrection of any form reveals over and over the nature of God living with the nature of humankind. Liturgy is a medium of that living. Liturgy which does not respect the integrity of its material disjoints the living. Liturgy which does, creates a chance for love anyone can choose.

Notes

1. International Commission on English in the Liturgy, Brief on the Liturgical Psalter: Pilot Study on a Liturgical Psalter (Feb 1982), Washington, DC, 7-12.

2. F. Sullivan, Poetic Psalms, *The Bible Today* (March 1981) pp. 121-126.

3. See J.-P. Manigne *Pour une poétique de la foi* (Paris 1969) p. 45. Also, H.-G. Gadamer *Truth and Method* (London 1975) pp. 345-447.

4. See H. Marcuse *The Aesthetic Dimension* (Boston 1978) III & V. Also, G. Durand *L'Imagination symbolique* (Paris 1968) pp. 34-35.

5. I am deeply influenced in this by Burton Raffel *The Forked Tongue. A Study of the Translation Process* (The Hague 1971) pp. 11-23, 160, 163-176: 'The challenge to me, as translator and poet, is to make—to discover really—an englished incarnation which I can then possess without dimunition.'

6. M. Dahood. *Psalms II (51-100)* The Anchor Bible (Vol. 17) (Garden City, New York 1960) pp. 301-307.

7. For an excellent study of poetic structures, as structures, and their power to intimate transcendent meaning, cf. J. G. Lawler *Celestial Pantomime: Poetic Structures of Transcendence* (New Haven 1979).

8. H. Gardner *Religion and Literature* (New York 1971) p. 131 re: traditional religious forms which go beyond judgments about quality.

9. See Peter Levi *The English Bible 1534-1859* (Grand Rapids 1974) pp. 9-41.

10. See D. Rosenberg *Blues of the Sky* (New York 1976) pp. 47-53. D. Berrigan *Uncommon Prayer. A Book of Psalms* (New York 1978).

11. See P. Evodokimov *L'Art de l'icône: théologie de la beauté* (Paris 1972) p. 199. What is said there of the icon refers also to the psalm-poem.

12. D. Sölle *Imagination et obéissance* (Paris 1970).

José Aldazábal

The Liturgy Should Learn from the Young

MANY YOUNG people have a negative attitude to the liturgy as it is practised at the moment. This often takes the form of indifference, absence or silence. Even in those groups which practise their faith, there is often a feeling of unease and coldness about the celebration of the liturgy or at least about certain forms of it.

Throughout the Church in the Sixties and Seventies there was an impor-tant movement to revitalise the liturgy and adapt it to the young. Several dioceses —not to mention the very numerous individual initiatives—published reflections and guidelines. Youth Easter celebrations and prayer groups seem to have opened new horizons.

Here we want to summarise the attitude of young Christians to the liturgy and especially the attitude that the liturgy—the celebrating community—ought to take to the young and the lessons it needs to learn from them.

1. THE LITURGY THEY DO NOT WANT

The disenchantment of the young with the recently renewed liturgy of the Church is usually caused by various aspects of it which the young, who do not always feel the same way as adults, feel to be deficient.

(a) The lack of living community

Sometimes this is the aspect which makes the most negative impression on them, more than language or forms: the lack of a real community. They often feel depersonalised in the midst of a passive, anonymous assembly which celebrates without joy. And this is not just because they are not made welcome but because the atmosphere, rhythm, language and lack of active participation betray an unmotivated community which hardly exists outside the celebration. When there is a lively Christian community—in its mission of evangelisation and brotherhood—it is usually also lively in its celebration. It is not strange that the young should desert this kind of celebration. The 'lack of models' here is obvious.

(b) **They do not like the compulsory and the prefabricated**

When the basic drive of a celebration appears to be the 'precept' the young are instinctively put off. Dogmatism and ritualism are attitudes which clearly repel. Even when they appreciate to some extent the values of ecclesiality, they do not accept the stress frequently laid on the compulsory nature of the celebration.

Neither do they take to a celebration which is laid down and regulated in detail, even though they are told that this is the heritage of a tradition, however venerable. Outside a certain basic scheme—which they easily understand—obedience to liturgical rules (often badly presented or rigidly interpreted) seems to them the best way to kill a celebration.

(c) **An alien language**

Sometimes it is the content of the celebration, or at least its language, that leaves them cold.

Often the texts are too theologically technical and abstract. Could not the same be expressed in more accessible and expressive terms? Sometimes this feeling of alienation is caused by the faulty instruction or education (biblical, for example) of the young. But sometimes the fault clearly belongs to the liturgical language itself, which creates a barrier for the young, and for the adults too, and makes it difficult for them to share in the mystery. The translation of the liturgy into living languages did not do everything. We might say that this was the easiest part of the reform. It has also brought out a deeper problem, the need for a liturgical language which is better adapted to the spirituality of the Christian of today.

(d) **Little connection with life**

It is true that the Eucharist and the other sacraments and prayer are the action of God, initiated by Christ, a gift from above. But they should also connect with the community that is celebrating. And here the young accuse the liturgy of disconnection from life and history. People feel ths particulary strongly now. How is the celebration connected with the rest of life, with the large human problems, with the urgencies of socio-political history? Is the liturgy not too aseptic and colourless for those Christians vitally interested in this existential dimension of their faith? Should it not be less of a parenthesis and more of an expression and motive force of the life of faith? Many young people feel that our liturgy contains no echo of daily history: it has a tranquillising effect on the Christians who celebrate it and takes no notice of the important questions for people today.

2. VALUES THEY APPRECIATE

The values of celebration are the same for all but everyone, according to age, education, culture etc., appreciates some values more than others.

(a) **Authenticity of celebration**

Authenticity—or rather sincerity, truth—is not, unfortunately, an aspect which bothers adults very much in the celebration. Through a defective education they have learnt to go along with lifeless celebrations whose signs and gestures lack expressiveness and truth.

The young feel differently: they intuitively feel the need of more authentic signs, a

Word of God truly 'celebrated' and not just ritually received, some symbolic gestures—like the kiss of peace or the greeting—which are more expressive of what they mean to signify.

They seek a celebration more firmly based on conviction than on the authority of tradition or the norm. They accept the elements the reason of which for being there they understand.

Is this not what the Council had in mind when it said that efforts should be directed 'not only towards seeing that the rules for a valid and lawful celebration are observed, but also that the faithful share in it in a conscious, active and fruitful manner' (SC 11), in accordance with their age, state, mode of life, level of religious education (SC 19)?

(b) The sense of community

As well as the affirmation of their own personality the young also appreciate belonging to the group and its communal action.

Their experience of prayer and the sacraments is mostly linked to the experience of the Christian group. They dislike massification and seek a smaller, more homogenous group. They want an atmosphere of sharing their faith and celebration, a feeling of welcome. They want to be protagonists and not merely spectators. This feeling also has the backing of the Council with its stress on participation and the new perspective of the 'celebrating community' offered by the liturgical books themselves.

(c) Greater creativity

Celebrations should not be based on a defensive and conservative attitude which merely repeats given formulae. It should be a re-creation. Liturgical books— instruments which are both relative and necessary to bring about the new event of a celebration—are only valid for the young up to a certain point. Just as the 'Directory of Masses for Children' offers a wide margin of flexibility in the means to be used for achieving the aims of the celebration in its various stages, it is also reasonable that the young should want their own language in an atmosphere of creativity.

It is true of course that the liturgy cannot be invented every time because it has a nucleus of content and ecclesial formulae which are given. But this should not be a justification for total rigidity. It is not strange that the young should seek more spontaneity, particularity, intimacy and expressiveness, so that the celebration may be more festive and creative.

3. NEW EXPERIENCES

In recent years there has been a series of movements of spirituality among the young. These have a strong effect on their relation to the liturgy.

(a) New taste for the contemplative and gratuitous

Phenomena like Taizé and many other centres of spirituality force us to take seriously the capacity of the young of today for prayer and contemplation. For many of them this capacity remained latent until they came into contact with living models of religious experience and then it proved to be very much alive.

It is not right to try and attribute the strength of this attraction to novelty or snobbery. The experience has proved too deep to make it possible to deny its validity. Sometimes it involves a rejection of the more institutionalised forms of the liturgy. But at the same time there is a rediscovery of the values of contemplation, gratuitousness, depth of prayer and a more authentic and festive celebration. As their Christian faith matures, many young people have clearly chosen to make the person of Jesus Christ and the living power of God's word the centre of their lives, as the Council clearly proposed.

(b) Confirmation, a faith which makes a commitment

A strongly 'catechumenal' trend has arisen in the Church, especially around the sacrament of Cofirmation.

While in no way forgetting the nature of this sacrament as the Gift of the Spirit, the catechetical approach in preparation for it has made many of the young understand their faith as a personal choice in response to this Gift, as a way and a search rather than a reality already attained, a commitment rather than an isolated celebration. And all this is a communal experience in the group. This has a strong influence on other areas of their religious life.

(c) Fascination with the East

Another interesting phenomenon, especially for the young of the western world, is the attraction of eastern spirituality especially in the form of Zen, yoga and transcendental meditation.

Many elements of this influence can be considered positive: the value given to the inner life, inner liberation of the senses, power of concentration, exercise of the potential of the human body for expressiveness, the taste for silence and contemplation, openness to the divine and the transcendental, the acceptance of a spiritual guide. . . .

True, other aspects are questionable in relation to more specifically Christian values: the perception of the divinity as impersonal and cosmic rather than as personal in Christ; the difference between the group experience of these movements and the characteristics of the ecclesial community; the stress on human techniques of access to the divine. . . .

But this is certainly a trend which forces Christians to consider the question whether it is simply a fascination with the exotic, or the search for values which are neglected in our western civilisation and our liturgies?

(d) Youth Easter celebrations

Beginning with Taizé there has been a growing trend in many places to hold Easter celebrations for the young. These can be considered as symptomatic of the search for depth of faith, personal choices, authenticity in celebration and symbolic expressiveness.

Apart from certain deficiencies, I believe these Easter celebrations to have a positive value. It is a new style of faith and celebration which will certainly influence the young and the rest of the community through a more creative and imaginative liturgy.

4. EXPLICABLE DEFICIENCIES

Besides these positive and promising trends, the young also show certain deficiencies, which are largely explicable by their psychology and life-style.

(a) Their *sense of tradition* is not very highly developed. They have no past, only a present and a future. The weight and argument of tradition does not instil them with the

G

same respect as it does their elders. They require a gradual initiation into a sense of tradition.

(b) Their *sense of the Church* as the institutional community, both local and universal, is also weak.

(c) There is also the *danger of superficiality and subjectivism*. The content of the Christian celebration should be clearly expressed: the mystery of Christ, the signs of the Covenant, the Word of God, God's free action by grace. . . .

But it is difficult for all Christians, especially the young, to reach this level of profundity. If they are not well instructed in the dynamic of the celebration, they may remain at the superficial level of music, atmosphere, symbolic gestures etc., or be concerned only with the emotional tone of the celebration, the friendliness and dialogue.

(d) *Difficult perseverance*. Many groups which begin with enthusiasm only last a very short time, especially if they have no depth of faith and no demanding programme. The natural instability and mirage-like qualities of the easy media—music, atmosphere etc. . . . do not answer their highest aspirations and this leads to a falling off of their creative will. Then another of their attitudes is likely to cause problems. This is their perfectionism which leads them only to approve of their kind of celebration and to see no value in a more communal gathering. They must learn to understand the differences between people and the way in which they could contribute to bringing more vitality to the adult assemblies, and not shut themselves up in spiritual narcissism.

5. LESSONS FOR THE LITURGY OF THE FUTURE

The Church must accept the challenge of these young people to the liturgy. It must take the criticism seriously and consider what it can do in the future.

(a) Acceptance of pluralism

Here this means showing confidence in the intentions of these youthful groups and overcoming the deep suspicion felt towards them by many adults. We complain that the young 'don't come'. But when at last they do come—in their own way, naturally, not our way—we complain about their style of faith or celebration.

It is a pity that phenomena such as the Youth Easter celebrations, which are usually full of undeniable value, are so often treated in a defensive and critical way, both by officials and individuals. Discernment is necessary and this is indeed one of the best ways of seeking the good of the young: helping them to see the value and what is unsuitable. But if we start by putting every creative attempt under the microscope of theological orthodoxy and subject it to a rubricist norm, we condemn to failure the small dose of hope and imagination still remaining in the young and the pastors closest to them. At the very least we have to make sure that the Christian community accepts the plurality of styles in its liturgical celebration.

(b) A more creative liturgy

The new provisions of the recent reform have not been accompanied by the necessary instruction or creative activation of participation by the celebrating assembly. This gives a feeling of poverty to the general tone of the celebration.

On the one hand education is necessary so that people understand the dynamics of the celebration and the reason why its various elements are there (psalms, sacramental signs, eucharistic prayer etc.). But on the other hand it also requires a brave and imaginative effort by the Church to adapt the liturgy into a key of more creative flexibility. The language of many texts is unsuitable: it could come much closer to the style of the young without at all impoverishing the mystery being celebrated. This could be done on the same lines as the adaptation of masses for children or the work done by writers of liturgical books for areas with different languages. It cannot be said that the possibilities for children's liturgy in the Directory of 1973 we have already mentioned have been followed up with great continuity: they were greeted with suspicion when it came to practical application. We believe that this would also be the most realistic and pastorally appropriate way for the young as they seek a more pleasant set-up for their celebration, a more intimate form of participation, a better adaptation to their psychology, the role of protagonists in the celebration while maintaining all due respect to the value of the various ministries, especially that of the president.

If those responsible for the Christian community had been more aware of what was lacking they could have done something about it. Of course the attempt at creative adaptation must be able to cope with all the various aspects that enter into the liturgy: the tension between the gift of God and the expression of individual faith; personal experience of ecclesial categories; the unchanging nucleus with more variable elements; respect for the principle of 'ex opere operato' along with doing justice to the anthropological. . . . But this should not become an 'alibi' for inaction or for an attitude of distrust and lamentation. We all know the dangers to be avoided. A botched youth liturgy could impoverish its content by confusing it with other levels, which may be good but which do not respect the identity of the Christian celebration. But as well as trying to avoid these ills, we must recognise that we still have a long way to go in the reform begun by the Council until we reach a more authentic and living form of celebration.

(c) Liturgy in a global life project

Another valid point which youthful ideas bring to the liturgy is the need to connect it with the global process of Christian life, and not to think of the liturgy as something done in isolation from the rest of life.

Sometimes the liturgy is criticised for lack of preparation, the Gospel has not been preached enough and people go on to the sacraments in very doubtful conditions of Christian faith. At other times the criticism is of the liturgy's lack of consequences: celebrations that have nothing to do with the real life behaviour of those who take part in them. In the case of Confirmation—we leave aside here discussion of the usefulness of giving the sacrament to the young—there has been a growing realisation of the value of a catechumenal approach to the sacrament which looks at it as a personal choice to bear witness and to take a greater part in the life of the Church.

Is not what the liturgy lacks today the fulfilment seen as necessary by the Council when it moved from the too pan-liturgical view of *Sacrosanctum Concilium* to the more solid perspective of the new ecclesiology in *Lumen Gentium* and openness towards mission and involvement in the world with *Gaudium et Spes*? Many Christian communities lack this global Christian dimension. This should be centred in the growth of a living community, not only taken up with its own celebrations—although of course these are important—but in all the areas of its mission, as we see illustrated in Acts in the case of the Christian community in Jerusalem. And this is the most valid part of the accusation made by the young against a liturgy which is too disconnected and uninvolved and which has no conscious and active community as its base.

(d) Margin for symbolic creativity

The liturgy of today has been accused of being too rational and verbalist (the 'religion of the book'). In the Third World, and also among the young, efforts are being made to make what should be the specific language of the liturgy more expressive: the symbolic action. This is the most intuitive, poetic and universal mode of expression: 'performative' signs which introduce us into the mystery and help to give us access to the transcendental: God's action and the saving presence of Christ in the celebration.

After a series of historical developments in which the Church valiantly assumed symbolic elements from different cultures, it seems that we have now entered a phase of being afraid to create a more imaginative symbolism. Most of the classical symbols are still valid, especially if they are well presented. But our generation should also be creative in this way: and it is the young who can show us how.

If we look at the Easter celebrations for the young, we see how their preferred mode of expression is the symbolic and we can only admire the imagination with which they translate the fundamental values of what they are celebrating and the attitudes that derive from them into this language of symbols. Although some may not work perfectly, most of them appear to unite instruction with respect for the central intention of the rite. With the necessary discernment but also with confidence, we should be grateful to the young for this attitude of creative imagination which could help us emerge from the tone of rational celebration, more catechetic than liturgical, into which the official liturgy has partly fallen.

6. CONCLUSION

Taking care of the young should not be a secondary matter in the pastoral work of the Church. They are a real force, a reality now—and not just because in them lies the future of the Church—which merits attention and respect.

The fact that they are often absent or critical of the community celebration should not surprise us too much. We find a symptomatic event in the Sunday assembly at Troas (Acts 20): it was a young man who fell asleep during St Paul's preaching and fell out of the window. . . . We should give a measure of confidence to the youthful style of celebration, at the same time helping them not to stray pedagogically or theologically too far away from the structure of the liturgy and to become more mature in their faith. But we should also leave them the freedom to adopt their own style of celebratory expression.

It would also be wise for the community to accept the lessons that can be learned from the young in all celebrations and try to make them more lively and festive, participatory and authentic. We should accept what is positive in the criticisms of the young because they often put their finger on obvious deficiences. Let us hope that these same young people will help to improve parish masses by their example and thus become the chief leaven of the community. We should regard the challenge made by the young and their experience of livelier celebrations as a constructive criticism of other celebrations, which do not achieve an atmosphere of active participation. The Christian community would do well to listen to this criticism and consider how it affects celebrating priest, the place of celebration, the language itself of the liturgy and the attitudes and behaviour of the community.

Christian young people are also the Church. I do not know whether they are the nucleus and the factor which will transform history. But I know that this cannot happen without them. As in society young people today have a lot to learn about life. But also a lot to teach.

Translated by Dinah Livingstone

Contributors

JOSÉ ALDAZÁBAL was born in Azkoitia (Gipuzkoa, Spain) in 1933. He belongs to the Congregation of Salesian Fathers and was ordained priest in 1958. In his studies his special subject was liturgy and in 1970 he defended his doctoral thesis in Rome on 'The ecclesiological doctrine of the Liber Orationum Psalmographus', published in Rome in 1974. He is on the editorial board of and writes for the youth pastoral care review *Mission Joven* (Madrid). He belongs to the Centre de Pastoral Liturgica, Barcelona, and has collaborated in their publications *Phase, Oracion de las Horas, Misa Dominical*. He is editor of the collection *Dossiers CPL*. His main publications are: *Ritmo joven del año cristiano* (Madrid 1971), *Eucaristia con jovenes* (Madrid 1974), *Claves para la oracion* (Barcelona 1981), and *Veinte siglos de oracion y diez años de reforma* (Madrid 1981).

MARY COLLINS, OSB, was born in 1935, and studied at the Catholic University in Washington, DC, receiving her doctorate in 1967. Since 1978 she has been associate professor of religion and religious education at that university. She is an associate editor of *Worship*, has served as a consultant to the International Commission on English in the Liturgy, and is presently a co-director of *Concilium*.

JOSEPH GELINEAU, SJ, born in France in 1920, is parish priest of five rural parishes in the Paris region. He has spent thirty years working for liturgical renewal as a composer, a teacher (Catholic Institute in Paris), a writer, as a member of the Roman *Consilium* for the implementation of liturgical reforms and the French National Pastoral Liturgy Centre, and as co-founder of the international research group for singing and music in liturgy *Universa Laus*.

CHARLES PERROT, who was born in 1929, is a priest of the diocese of Moulin in central France. He has been a seminary professor since 1955. In 1960 he began teaching oriental languages at the Facultés Catholiques at Lyons before in 1969 becoming a professor at the Institut Catholique in Paris. At present he teaches New Testament exegesis (St Paul) and Syriac at the Institute's school of oriental languages. Among his books are: *La Lecture de la Bible dans la synagogue. Les anciennes lectures palestiniennes du Shabbat et des fêtes* (1973); with P. M. Bogaert editor of Pseudo-Philo, *Livre des Antiquités Bibliques* (Sources chrétiennes 230) (1976); *Introduction á la Bible* (èdition nouvelle), III:2, (Les Actes des Apôtres) (1976); *Jésus et l'histoire* (1979).

CHARLES PIETRI was born in Marseilles in 1932, studied at the Ecole Normale Supérieure and was a member of the French School at Rome. He is currently professor of the history of Christianity at the university of Paris-Sorbonne and director of the Nain de Tillemont centre founded by H. I. Marrou for research into early Christianity and late antiquity. His principal publication is *Roma Christiana: recherches sur l'Eglise de Rome, son organisation, sa politique, son idéologie de Miltiade à Sixte III (311-440)* (1976)

PAUL PUTHANANGADY, SDB, was born in 1934 in Kerala, India, joined the Salesians (SDB) in 1953; did his theological studies in Italy and was ordained in Turin in 1964; did his post-graduate studies in the Pontifical Athenaeum of St Anselm in Rome and obtained a doctorate in theology with specialisation in liturgy. At present he is the director of the National, Biblical and Liturgical Centre and the Editor of *Word and Worship*. He has published many articles on liturgy and sacraments in various theological reviews. His last published work is a book on liturgy—*Initiation to Christian Worship*.

TITIANMA ANSELME SANON was born in 1937 at Bobo-Dioulasso in Upper Volta. He was ordained priest in 1962. He obtained a degree in dogmatic theology at the Gregorian University in Rome in 1966, a degree in sociology at the Hautes Etudes, Paris, in 1967, and a doctorate in theology from the Catholic Institute of Paris on 'Third Church, my Mother, or the conversion of a pagan community to Christ' (Bobo-Dioulasso 1970). He was a teacher at the seminary of Koumi in Upper Volta, then rector, until his nomination as Bishop of Bobo-Dioulasso in 1974. Published articles have appeared in *Afrique et Parole, Cahiers d'Etudes Africaines, Christus, Concilium, Lumière et Vie, La Maison Dieu, Mission de L'Eglise, Misiones Extranjeras, Revue du Clergé africain, Spiritus, Eelema*, and he made a communication to the Toulouse Symposium on 'The Humanity of the Eucharist'.

PEDRO FARNES SCHERER was born in Barcelona in 1925 and ordained there in 1950, studying in Barcelona, Rome and Paris. He is a founder member of the Centre for Pastoral Liturgy in Barcelona, and on the editorial committees of *Phase* (Barcelona) and *Actualidad litúrgica* (Mexico), as well as adviser to the Bishops' Liturgical Conferences of Spain, Mexico, Colombia, and CELAM. His published works include books on the general ordering of the Roman Missal, the place for celebration and the prayer of the Hours for the faithful.

FRANCIS P. SULLIVAN gained the degrees of AB, AM(Phil) at Boston College, USA; and of STD at the Institut Catholique de Paris. He is currently lecturer in theology at Boston College, USA, giving courses on Imagination and Religious Understanding. He is also visiting professor at the Gregorian University, Rome. He is author of two volumes of poetry, *Table Talk with the Recent God* (New York), and *Spy Wednesday's Kind* (New York), and of articles on aesthetics and theology in various journals.

HERMAN WEGMAN was born in 1930 and is at present professor of the history of liturgy and dogmatics in the Catholic Theological University of Utrecht, the Netherlands. He studied in Rome and Paris (1955-1960) and graduated in 1960 with a study of *Pâques du premier jour au huitième*. Among other things, he has written a history of Christian worship in the East, *Geschiedenis van de christelijke eredienst in het Oosten* (1976), which was published in English in 1982. At the moment, he is working on a study of comparative heortology, which will involve the writing of a book on the subject.

JAMES F. WHITE was born in Boston, Massachusetts in 1932. He is father of five children and has taught Christian worship at Perkins School of Theology, Southern

Methodist University, Dallas, Texas, since 1961. He is an United Methodist minister, chaired for a number of years the editorial committee of the United Methodist Supplemental Worship Resources project, and is past president of the North American Academy of Liturgy. His books include: *The Cambridge Movement, Protestant Worship and Church Architecture, The Worldliness of Worship, New Forms of Worship, Christian Worship in Transition,* and *Introduction to Christian Worship.*

CONCILIUM

1. (Vol. 1 No. 1) **Dogma.** Ed. Edward Schillebeeckx. 86pp.
2. (Vol. 2 No. 1) **Liturgy.** Ed. Johannes Wagner. 100pp.
3. (Vol. 3 No. 1) **Pastoral.** Ed. Karl Rahner. 104pp.
4. (Vol. 4 No. 1) **Ecumenism.** Hans Küng. 108pp.
5. (Vol. 5 No. 1) **Moral Theology.** Ed. Franz Bockle 98pp.
6. (Vol. 6 No. 1) **Church and World.** Ed. Johannes Baptist Metz. 92pp.
7. (Vol. 7 No. 1) **Church History.** Roger Aubert. 92pp.
8. (Vol. 8 No. 1) **Canon Law.** Ed. Teodoro Jimenez Urresti and Neophytos Edelby. 96pp.
9. (Vol. 9 No. 1) **Spirituality.** Ed. Christian Duquoc. 88pp.
10. (Vol. 10 No. 1) **Scripture.** Ed. Pierre Benoit and Roland Murphy. 92pp.
11. (Vol. 1 No. 2) **Dogma.** Ed. Edward Schillebeeckx. 88pp.
12. (Vol. 2 No. 2) **Liturgy.** Ed. Johannes Wagner. 88pp.
13. (Vol. 3 No. 2) **Pastoral.** Ed. Karl Rahner. 84pp.
14. (Vol. 4 No. 2) **Ecumenism.** Ed. Hans Küng. 96pp.
15. (Vol. 5 No. 2) **Moral Theology.** Ed. Franz Bockle. 88pp.
16. (Vol. 6 No. 2) **Church and World.** Ed. Johannes Baptist Metz. 84.pp.
17. (Vol. 7 No. 2) **Church History.** Ed. Roger Aubert. 96pp.
18. (Vol. 8 No. 2) **Religious Freedom.** Ed. Neophytos Edelby and Teodoro Jimenez Urresti. 96pp.
19. (Vol. 9 No. 2) **Religionless Christianity?** Ed. Christian Duquoc. 96pp.
20. (Vol. 10 No. 2) **The Bible and Tradition.** Ed. Pierre Benoit and Roland E. Murphy. 96pp.
21. (Vol. 1 No 3) **Revelation and Dogma.** Ed. Edward Schillebeeckx. 88pp.
22. (Vol. 2 No. 3) **Adult Baptism and Initiation.** Ed. Johannes Wagner. 96pp.
23. (Vol. 3 No. 3) **Atheism and Indifference.** Ed. Karl Rahner. 92pp.
24. (Vol. 4 No. 3) **The Debate on the Sacraments.** Ed. Hans Küng. 92pp.
25. (Vol. 5 No. 3) **Morality, Progress and History.** Ed. Franz Bockle. 84pp.
26. (Vol. 6 No. 3) **Evolution.** Ed. Johannes Baptist Metz. 88pp.
27. (Vol. 7 No. 3) **Church History.** Ed. Roger Aubert. 92pp.
28. (Vol. 8 No. 3) **Canon Law—Theology and Renewal.** Ed. Neophytos Edelby and Teodoro Jimenez Urresti. 92pp.
29. (Vol. 9 No. 3) **Spirituality and Politics.** Ed. Christian Duquoc. 84pp.
30. (Vol. 10 No. 3) **The Value of the Old Testament.** Ed. Pierre Benoit and Roland Murphy. 92pp.
31. (Vol. 1 No. 4) **Man, World and Sacrament.** Ed. Edward Schillebeeckx. 84pp.
32. (Vol. 2 No. 4) **Death and Burial: Theology and Liturgy.** Ed. Johannes Wagner. 88pp.
33. (Vol. 3 No. 4) **Preaching the Word of God.** Ed. Karl Rahner. 96pp.
34. (Vol. 4 No. 4) **Apostolic by Succession?** Ed. Hans Küng. 96pp.

35. (Vol. 5 No. 4) **The Church and Social Morality.** Ed. Franz Bockle. 92pp.
36. (Vol. 6 No. 4) **Faith and the World of Politics.** Ed. Johannes Baptist Metz 96pp.
37. (Vol. 7 No. 4) **Prophecy.** Ed. Roger Aubert. 80pp.
38. (Vol. 8 No. 4) **Order and the Sacraments.** Ed. Neophytos Edelby and Teodoro Jimenez Urresti. 96pp.
39. (Vol. 9 No. 4) **Christian Life and Eschatology.** Ed. Christian Duquoc. 94pp.
40. (Vol. 10 No. 4) **The Eucharist: Celebrating the Presence of the Lord.** Ed. Pierre Benoit and Roland Murphy. 88pp.
41. (Vol. 1 No. 5) **Dogma.** Ed. Edward Schillebeeckx. 84pp.
42. (Vol. 2 No. 5) **The Future of the Liturgy.** Ed. Johannes Wagner. 92pp.
43. (Vol. 3 No. 5) **The Ministry and Life of Priests Today.** Ed. Karl Rahner. 104pp.
44. (Vol. 4 No. 5) **Courage Needed.** Ed. Hans Küng. 92pp.
45. (Vol. 5 No. 5) **Profession and Responsibility in Society.** Ed. Franz Bockle. 84pp.
46. (Vol. 6 No. 5) **Fundamental Theology.** Ed. Johannes Baptist Metz. 84pp.
47. (Vol. 7 No. 5) **Sacralization in the History of the Church.** Ed. Roger Aubert. 80pp.
48. (Vol. 8 No. 5) **The Dynamism of Canon Law.** Ed. Neophytos Edelby and Teodoro Jimenez Urresti. 92pp.
49. (Vol. 9 No. 5) **An Anxious Society Looks to the Gospel.** Ed. Christian Duquoc. 80pp.
50. (Vol. 10 No. 5) **The Presence and Absence of God.** Ed. Pierre Benoit and Roland Murphy. 88pp.
51. (Vol. 1 No. 6) **Tension between Church and Faith.** Ed. Edward Schillebeeckx. 160pp.
52. (Vol. 2 No. 6) **Prayer and Community.** Ed. Herman Schmidt. 156pp.
53. (Vol. 3 No. 6) **Catechetics for the Future.** Ed. Alois Müller. 168pp.
54. (Vol. 4 No. 6) **Post-Ecumenical Christianity.** Ed. Hans Küng. 168pp.
55. (Vol. 5 No. 6) **The Future of Marriage as Institution.** Ed. Franz Bockle. 180pp.
56. (Vol. 6 No. 6) **Moral Evil Under Challenge.** Ed. Johannes Baptist Metz. 160pp.
57. (Vol. 7 No. 6) **Church History at a Turning Point.** Ed. Roger Aubert. 160pp.
58. (Vol. 8 No. 6) **Structures of the Church's Presence in the World of Today.** Ed. Teodoro Jimenez Urresti. 160pp.
59. (Vol. 9 No. 6) **Hope.** Ed. Christian Duquoc. 160pp.
60. (Vol. 10 No. 6) **Immortality and Resurrection.** Ed. Pierre Benoit and Roland Murphy. 160pp.
61. (Vol. 1 No. 7) **The Sacramental Administration of Reconciliation.** Ed. Edward Schillebeeckx. 160pp.
62. (Vol. 2 No. 7) **Worship of Christian Man Today.** Ed. Herman Schmidt. 156pp.
63. (Vol. 3 No. 7) **Democratization of the Church.** Ed. Alois Müller. 160pp.

64. (Vol. 4 No. 7) **The Petrin Ministry in the Church.** E Hans Küng. 160pp.
65. (Vol. 5 No. 7) **The Manip of Man.** Ed. Franz Bockle 144pp.
66. (Vol. 6 No. 7) **Fundamen Theology in the Church.** Johannes Baptist Metz. 1
67. (Vol. 7 No. 7) **The Self-Understanding of the Church.** Ed. Roger Aube 144pp.
68. (Vol. 8 No. 7) **Contestatic the Church.** Ed. Teodoro Jimenez Urresti. 152pp.
69. (Vol. 9 No. 7) **Spirituality Public or Private?** Ed. Ch Duquoc. 156pp.
70. (Vol. 10 No. 7) **Theology Exegesis and Proclamatio** Roland Murphy. 144pp.
71. (Vol. 1 No. 8) **The Bisho the Unity of the Church.** Edward Schillebeeckx. 15
72. (Vol. 2 No. 8) **Liturgy an Ministry.** Ed. Herman Sc 160pp.
73. (Vol. 3 No. 8) **Reform of Church.** Ed. Alois Mülle Norbert Greinacher. 152
74. (Vol. 4 No. 8) **Mutual Recognition of Ecclesial Ministries?** Ed. Hans Kü Walter Kasper. 152pp.
75. (Vol. 5 No. 8) **Man in a** Society. Ed. Franz Bockle 160pp.
76. (Vol. 6 No. 8) **The God Question.** Ed. Johannes B Metz. 156pp.
77. (Vol. 7 No. 8) **Election-Consensus-Reception.** Ed. Giuseppe Alberigo and A Weiler. 156pp.
78. (Vol. 8 No. 8) **Celibacy c Catholic Priest.** Ed. Willi Bassett and Peter Huizin 160pp.
79. (Vol. 9 No. 8) **Prayer.** Ed Christian Duquoc and Cl Geffré. 126pp.
80. (Vol. 10 No. 8) **Ministrie Church.** Ed. Bas van Iers Roland Murphy. 152pp.
81. **The Persistence of Religic** Andrew Greeley and Gre Baum. 0 8164 2537 X 16
82. **Liturgical Experience of** Ed. Herman Schmidt and Power. 0 8164 2538 8 14
83. **Truth and Certainty.** Ed. Edward Schillebeeckx an van Iersel. 0 8164 2539 6
84. **Political Commitment an Christian Community.** Ed Müller and Norbert Grei 0 8164 2540 X 156pp.
85. **The Crisis of Religious L** Ed. Johannes Baptist Me Jean-Pierre Jossua. 0 8164 2541 8 144pp.
86. **Humanism and Christian** Claude Geffré. 0 8164 25 144pp.
87. **The Future of Christian Marriage.** Ed. William K and Peter Huizing. 0 8164 2575 2
88. **Polarization in the Chur** Hans Küng and Walter K 0 8164 2572 8 156pp.
89. **Spiritual Revivals.** Ed. C Duquoc and Casiano Fle 0 8164 2573 6 156pp.
90. **Power and the Word of** Ed. Franz Bockle and Ja Marie Pohier. 0 8164 2574 4 156pp.